Preface

Jamestown Rediscovery VI is the sixth booklet in a series of yearly updates on the historical and archaeological research known as *Jamestown Rediscovery*, carried out under the auspices of the Association for the Preservation of Virginia Antiquities on its 22.5 acres on Jamestown Island. From the outset, there were two major goals for the project: (1)find, uncover, and recover whatever might remain of the earliest settlement and the growth of the 17th-century town *and,* at the same time, (2)make that process of discovery as accessible to the visiting public as possible. For that reason the site and related laboratory work is as visitor friendly as it can be, and considerable staff effort has gone into publishing the results of the research in a timely manner. Part of that publishing program is the *Rediscovery* series, which is literally rushed into print before the excitement of discovery fades. The down side of such a rapid publication program is that the time for full analysis to support conclusions is constricted, and therefore the meaning of discoveries is always subject to change through time. Therefore the reader should be advised that what appears in print every year is not necessarily a *conclusion* but rather a *working theory* to be tested during future research. That, of course, is not really any different then any attempt to reconstruct and understand the past. However, the yearly deadline here distills the process and renders most attempts to breath meaning into the discoveries all the more tentative.

Acknowledgements:

The authors wish to gratefully acknowledge the support and efforts of the following organizations and individuals:

The Association for the Preservation of Virginia Antiquities, especially Martin Kirwan King, President, and Peter Dun Grover, Executive Director.

The Commonwealth of Virginia

The National Endowment for the Humanities

The National Geographic Society

For the support of Yeardley House Archaeological Center, Mr. and Mrs. John H. Cronly III, Mr. and Mrs. William M. Grover, Jr., Mrs. John H. Guy, Jr., Mr. and Mrs. James W. Rawles and the The Mary Morton Parsons Foundation

The National Society Colonial Daughters of the Seventeenth Century

The National Society Daughters of the Founders and Patriots of Virginia

Patricia Cornwell

The Colonial National Historical Park, National Park Service, Superintendent Alec Gould

Jamestown Rediscovery Advisory Board: Dr. Warren M. Billings, chairman, Dr. Dennis B. Blanton, Dr. Jeffrey P. Brain, Dr. Cary Carson, Dr. Kathleen Deagan, Dr. James Deetz, Dr. Rex M. Ellis, Dr. Alaric Faulkner, Dr. William W. Fitzhugh, Ms. Camille Hedrick, Dr. James Horn, Dr. Jon Kukla, Dr. Douglas Owsley, Dr. David Orr, Mr. Oliver Perry, Dr. Carmel Schrire, Dr. George Stuart, Dr. Sandra Treadway, Dr. Edwin Randolph Turner, Mr. Robert Wharton, Ms. Martha Williams.

Staff: The Rediscovery Project has been very much a team effort from the start and now very much an experienced team effort. With an open mind to ways of improving the process, over the initial 5 years of the project, the staff has had the opportunity to ever fine tune the way things have been done. I am especially grateful for their ability to together decipher the ever-widening archaeological story of Jamestown. I am indebted to curator Bly Straube's superior and ever-growing understanding of post-medieval material culture; information technologist and conservator Elliott Jordan's mastery of the digital world and quality publication; field supervisor Eric Deetz' growing insight into post-medieval vernacular architecture and his unique ability to educate visitors; graphic artist/archaeologist Jamie May's superior eye for beauty on the computer and for *reading* the mystery of archaeological soil; field supervisor Seth Mallios' tenacious search for archaeological meaning and tremendous research energy; conservator/photographer Michael Lavin's ever more uniquely experienced conservation touches and photographic eye; and for office manager/research assistant Catherine Correll-Wall's talent for so delicately balancing the ever-more complicated project schedule and at the same time beginning to *find* the original Jamestown settlers.

1999 Crew: Heather Lapham, Daniel Schmidt, Shane Emmet, Courtney Jamieson, Carter Hudgins, Jr., Martha Gates, Ernelyn Marx, Elizabeth Grzymala.

1999 Field School: Beth Barnes, Jami Lynn Bryan, Ellen Davis, Katherine Grillo, Adam Heinrich, Alexander Loscalzo, Ernelyn Marx, Eric Proebsting.

Volunteers: Don Ivey, Ted Wolf, Jessie McCulley, Alastair MacDonald, Ian MacDonald, Ranjith Jayasena, Andrew Deans.

For me, Ellen makes this all worthwhile.

WMK, Jamestown, Virginia, 4/12/2000.

Chapter 1

"104 Men and Boys..."

It was May 14, 1607. Just over 100 men and boys filed ashore from the *Susan Constant*, the *Godspeed*, and the *Discovery* onto what the English adventurers came to call Jamestown Island on the north shore of what they came to call the James River. Their decision to make that place the site of their Virginia settlement was no accident. They had spent over two and a half weeks searching for the proper setting for their town along the river from its mouth, at what they named Cape Henry and Cape Charles, inland to the confluence of the James and the Appomattox Rivers (present Hopewell). One eyewitness account simply explained that Jamestown Island was their choice because the channel came near enough to the shore to moor their ships to the trees.[1] That certainly made unloading supplies the least effort. But there was more to it than that. They had very specific instructions from the Virginia Company in England, the merchants and nobles who put up the money for the venture.[2] The Company officials had advised their charges to settle at least 100 miles from the ocean as protection from what they thought would surely be Spanish reprisals for English privateering raids and muscling in on "Spain's" New World. In fact, Jamestown Island was only 50 miles from the open sea. If they did settle closer to the ocean, the Virginia Company also advised the colonists to choose a naturally defensive place such as

Figure 1. Route of the James River exploration likely taken by the first settlers, April 29-May 13, 1607.

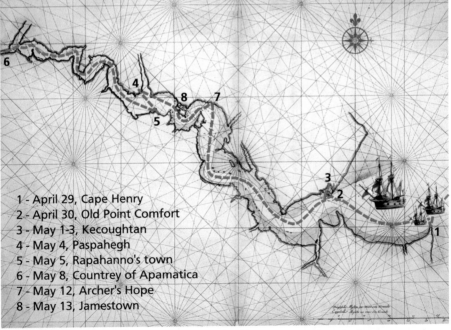

1 - April 29, Cape Henry
2 - April 30, Old Point Comfort
3 - May 1-3, Kecoughtan
4 - May 4, Paspahegh
5 - May 5, Rapahanno's town
6 - May 8, Countrey of Apamatica
7 - May 12, Archer's Hope
8 - May 13, Jamestown

"some Island." And to be politically sensitive they should choose a site not inhabited by the "naturals." Given those conditions there were few candidates for the settlement on the James River except Jamestown Island. While it was too close to the ocean, it nonetheless lay hidden from any approaching Spanish attack vessels behind a nearby peninsula the settlers named Hog Island.

That is the standard and less damning version of the siting of James Fort/James Towne at Jamestown Island. Usually descriptions of the marshy, mosquito-infested Island lacking fresh water are enough to prove how ignorant the decision was to settle in such an unhealthy place. Despite the fact that Jamestown turned out to be the durable beginning of what became the United States of America, most modern historians cannot emphasize enough how incompetent the leaders and their drone-like hundred plus followers were for choosing to establish the colony on that unwholesome piece of ground.[3] Except for a few scholars, most give major recognition for what little success Jamestown achieved to Captain John Smith, who left the most complete and only in-depth published account of the struggling early months of the venture. The rest of the party takes on the role of either minor supporting actors, names only, or shadowy "others unnamed." But in that chronicle Smith does give us 82 of the original settlers names and the names of those who arrived with the first and second supply ships in 1608. George Percy, destined to ultimately become resident Governor, also gives us some names. But his is not a happy

Figure 2. List of the names of the first settlers from Captain John Smith's Proceedings.

COUNCEL
Master Edward Maria Wingfield
Captaine Bartholomew Gosnoll
Captaine John Smith
Captaine John Ratliffe
Captaine John Martin
Captaine George Kendall

GENTLEMEN
Master Robert Hunt, Preacher
Master George Percie
Anthony Gosnoll
George Flower
Captaine Gabriell Archer
Robert Fenton
Robert Ford
William Bruster
Edward Harrington
Dru Pickhouse
Thomas Jacob
John Brookes
Ellis Kingston
Thomas Sands
Benjamin Beast
Jehu Robinson
Thomas Mouton
Eustace Clovill
Stephen Halthrop
Kellam Throgmorton
Edward Morish
Nathaniell Powell
Edward Browne

Robert Behethland
John Penington
Jeremy Alicock
George Walker
Thomas Studley
Richard Crofts
Nicholas Houlgrave
Thomas Webbe
John Waller
John Short
William Tankard
William Smethes
Francis Snarsbrough
Richard Simons
Edward Brookes
Richard Dixon
John Martin
Roger Cooke
Anthony Gosnold
Thomas Wotton,Chirurgian
John Stevenson
Thomas Gore
Henry Adling
Francis Midwinter
Richard Frith

CARPENTERS
William Laxon
Edward Pising
Thomas Emry
Robert Small

LABOURERS
John Laydon
William Cassen
George Cassen
Thomas Cassen
William Rodes
William White
Old Edward
Henry Tavin
George Goulding
John Dods
William Johnson
William Unger

James Read - Blacksmith
Jonas Profit - Sailer
Thomas Couper - Barber
William Garret - Bricklayer
Edward Brinto - Mason
William Love - Taylor
Nicholas Skot - Drummer
William Wickinson - Chiurgian

BOYS
Samuell Collier
Nathaniel Peacock
James Brumfield
Richard Mutton

WITH DIVERS OTHERS
John Herd - Bricklayer
Anas Todkill
John Capper
George Martin

list. It amounts to a death toll as he records the almost daily casualties of the grim days of August and September 1607. But at least the names of a good percentage of the people who first established the colony and some of those who died soon thereafter are known.[4] Now we can know more than names.

Jamestown archaeological excavations have so far recovered thousands of objects that these first Jamestonians brought with them and have begun to define the remains of the Fort and town they built. These are all clues to their Virginia lifestyle; clues to what it was like to be at Jamestown and clues that were thought lost for two centuries to James River shore erosion. But since 1994, more and more of the fallout of those first struggling years is coming to light. So, too, are telling documentary clues about exactly who these early settlers were and what experiences they brought with them from their previous lives in England. Until now, with the exception of a few of the leaders, the biographies of these first Anglo-Americans have remained a mystery. Genealogical research is beginning to unravel answers to questions like where the settlers were from in England, what lifestyle they left, how they knew about the venture in the first place, and why they came to Jamestown. Easily accessible digital records have now begun to dry up the ocean that separated interested American scholars from key documents scattered among English parish churches.[5]

But before seeking personal resumes of the adventurers from a time before they left England, we need to retrace their steps from where we left them: landing at Jamestown Island. Twenty days before choosing and landing at the Island and after the long-delayed passage, they first landed in Virginia at Cape Henry, in modern-day Virginia Beach. There the scouting party found abundant fresh water overflowing from innumerable springs. Perhaps assuming that these springs would be everywhere along the Virginia inland waterways, the expedition advanced upriver according to the instructions. Unfortunately the unplanned length of the voyage posed an unknown but fatal problem: when they ultimately arrived at Jamestown Island it was too late for meaningful planting. To make matters worse, the food supplies they brought along were either used up during the delayed crossing or rotten. It would take years to make up that food deficit, but it was particularly acute during that first summer.[6]

Continuing backward in time, it had been slightly over five months since the 144 settlers and sailors left England, but it is technically false that they embarked from London, as most history books state.[7] Rather they last trod on English soil at a place called Blackwall, slightly downriver from London and just below a foreboding sounding place known as the Isle of Dogs. Blackwall in the early-17th century consisted of alehouses and churches supporting the docks of the emerging English maritime trade. Today at the end of a street known as Blackwall Way is a place known traditionally as Blackwall stairs, where there exists the remnants of ap-

Figure 3. 1610 Map of London area showing Blackwall, the point of embarkation for the Jamestown settlers.

parently very old wooden stairs visible at lowtide. Local lore has it that the Virginia legion of men and boys boarded the three ships for Virginia there in that December of 1606. Nearby, and standing until at least 1897, was what the local historians call the Sir Walter Raleigh House, a Tudor half timber structure that served as an inn where travelers, presumably once Sir Walter himself, awaited transport out of the Thames.[8] This is conceivably the freshest memory of an English house that most of the future Jamestown settlers would carry with them during the tedious unending crossing to the New World. There must have been great longing to return to that rugged inn and the alehouses of Blackwall when the three

Figure 4. The "Sir Walter Raleigh House" at Blackwall, traditionally known for housing New World bound early explorers and settlers in the 16th and 17th centuries (demolished).

supposedly outbound ships lay stalled in bone chilling weather at the mouth of the Thames for over a month. Those who ever spent any length of time on airline runways waiting for the weather or traffic to clear can only begin to understand the feeling that these colonists must have experienced getting *nowhere* for almost half of the anticipated length of the voyage. But, again, exactly who were these shivering frustrated men and boys waiting for the winds and their fortunes to change?

Figure 5. Blackwall, England, dedication of an Association for the Preservation of Virginia Antiquities plaque commemorating the embarkation point of the Jamestown settlers, (1928). Inset, the American ambassador, Philip Lader, and Docklands, England, development officials dedicating a refurbished version of the earlier memorial, (1999).

Of course, certain biographical facts are commonly known about some of the Jamestown leaders. We know, for example, something of the members of the first council selected by the Virginia Company before the voyage and made known to the colonists when they opened a sealed box upon reaching the Virginia shore: Edward Maria Wingfield, John Martin, Captain George Kendall, John Ratcliffe, Bartholomew Gosnold, and Captain John Smith.[9] They all had military experience either acquired fighting the Spanish in the Netherlands or during the establishment of the English plantations in Ireland. Captain John Smith had the Dutch military experience in addition to fighting in France and Transylvania. They all were gentry except Smith, some urban and some rural. Their ages ranged from Wingfield, the oldest, who was approximately 47, to Smith, the youngest at 28. The rest of the Council were in their 40s, except Gosnold who was 36. They averaged close to 40. At a time when 56 was the average life expectancy, these men were primarily "seniors." [10] This may be yet another reason why the younger commoner Smith does not seem to fit in. The rest of the party, from which biographical data could be determined so far, ranged in age from the 52-year-old gentleman, Robert Pennington of London, to 14-year-old "boy" Richard Mutton, also of London. The average age of the non-council gentlemen and the group overall was about 30.[11]

The home parishes and probably the family seats of the group of settlers were overwhelmingly either the greater London area, including the

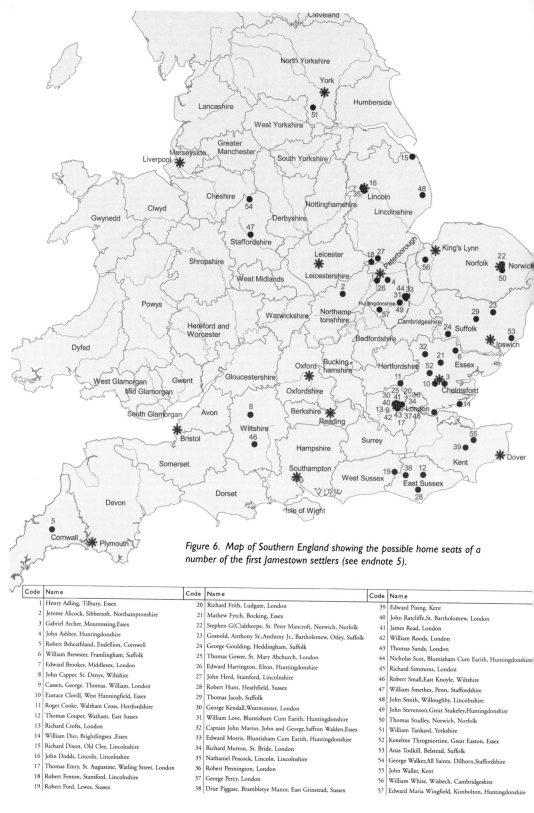

Figure 6. Map of Southern England showing the possible home seats of a number of the first Jamestown settlers (see endnote 5).

Code	Name
1	Henry Adling, Tilbury, Essex
2	Jerome Alicock, Sibbertoft, Northamptonshire
3	Gabriel Archer, Mountessing,Essex
4	John Ashbey, Huntingdonshire
5	Robert Beheathland, Endellion, Cornwell
6	William Brewster, Framlingham, Suffolk
7	Edward Brookes, Middlesex, London
8	John Capper, St. Denys, Wiltshire
9	Cassen, George, Thomas, William, London
10	Eustace Clovill, West Hanningfield, Essex
11	Roger Cooke, Waltham Cross, Hertfordshire
12	Thomas Couper, Watham, East Susses
13	Richard Crofts, London
14	William Dier, Brightlingsea ,Essex
15	Richard Dixon, Old Clee, Lincolnshire
16	John Dodds, Lincoln, Lincolnshire
17	Thomas Emry, St. Augustine, Watling Street, London
18	Robert Fenton, Stamford, Lincolnshire
19	Robert Ford, Lewes, Sussex

Code	Name
20	Richard Frith, Ludgate, London
21	Mathew Fytch, Bocking, Essex
22	Stephen G(C)althorpe, St. Peter Mancroft, Norwich, Norfolk
23	Gosnold, Anthony Sr.,Anthony Jr., Bartholemew, Otley, Suffolk
24	George Goulding, Heddingham, Suffolk
25	Thomas Gower, St. Mary Abchurch, London
26	Edward Harrington, Elton, Huntingdonshire
27	John Herd, Stamford, Lincolnshire
28	Robert Hunt, Heathfield, Sussex
29	Thomas Jacob, Suffolk
30	George Kendall, Westminster, London
31	William Love, Bluntisham Cum Earith, Huntingdonshire
32	Captain John Martin, John and George,Saffron Walden,Essex
33	Edward Morris, Bluntisham Cum Earith, Huntingdonshire
34	Richard Mutton, St. Bride, London
35	Nathaniel Peacock, Lincoln, Lincolnshire
36	Robert Pennington, London
37	George Percy, London
38	Drue Piggase, Brambletye Manor, East Grinstead, Sussex

Code	Name
39	Edward Pising, Kent
40	John Ratcliffe, St. Bartholomew, London
41	James Read, London
42	William Roods, London
43	Thomas Sands, London
44	Nicholas Scot, Bluntisham Cum Earith, Huntingdonshire
45	Richard Simmons, London
46	Robert Small,East Knoyle, Wiltshire
47	William Smethes, Penn, Staffordshire
48	John Smith, Willoughby, Lincolnshire
49	John Stevenson,Great Stukeley,Huntingdonshire
50	Thomas Studley, Norwich, Norfolk
51	William Tankard, Yorkshire
52	Kenelme Throgmortine, Great Easton, Essex
53	Anas Todkill, Belstead, Suffolk
54	George Walker,All Saints, Dilhorn,Staffordshire
55	John Waller, Kent
56	William White, Wisbech, Cambridgeshire
57	Edward Maria Wingfield, Kimbolton, Huntingdonshire

surrounding Kent, Sussex, and Essex counties; the Ipswich/Norwich areas of East Anglia; or the Peterborough area. The largest number of all the original colonists for which a place of origin could be possibly determined came from the city of London (16), but an equal number came from the greater London area and East Anglia. There seems to be a difference between the London area and East Anglia in ages at the time the Virginia fleet sailed, with the younger individuals coming from the river "port" town areas of Suffolk, Norfolk, Lincolnshire, and from Cambridgeshire. Only 11% came from any other town or county and not from any one other particular region in England. Fourteen came with relatives: cousins, fathers, sons, and brothers. Six had some kinship with Gosnold.[12]

From these statistics, admittedly determined from cursory research still in progress, one still might speculate how and why these men and boys wound up filing down those Blackwall stairs to begin their Virginia adventure. Of course, the prospect for finding gold was considered to be a realistic expectation. But there were also promises of assignments of land in Virginia to planters or adventurers.[13] It is logical to assume that many of the immigrants were the younger sons of gentry, with little prospects of inheriting the family lands in England. Where it can be determined from records so far, that was the case for at least six of the gentlemen and probably for a majority of the remaining 22, for whom older siblings could not be determined. For example, the gentleman Bartholmew Gosnold had an older brother, and Stephen Calthrope of Norfolk, who was a relative of the future Jamestown president, Wingfield, had two older brothers. Prospects for their acquiring land in Virginia must have been appealing to these younger gentlemen. That seems to have been true of immigrants well into the 17th century.[14] But surprisingly it seems that acquiring land could not be the primary consideration for many others. At least 13 other gentleman, including Wingfield and Martin, were the eldest sons in their families.[15] Clearly they were gentlemen with other motives, perhaps just the adventure in its own right.

But obviously the men and boys had to at least learn about the voyage before they could possibly sign on to go. How did the word get out in an age when only one in ten could read and where the roads were hardly passable? The distribution patterns of geographic origins may be a clue.[16] They suggest that getting the word out can be attributed to the principal leaders. It is logical to assume that the settlers from London simply learned of the venture through the promotional program of the Virginia Company based there. In fact, Gosnold's cousin was Thomas Smythe, the London merchant, "whose wealth and influence played so large a part in the formation of the first Virginia Company," and who may have had a personal hand in collecting the London recruits himself.[17] It is clear that Gosnold gathered the leaders and many of the other first settlers from

Figure 7. Otley Hall, Suffolk, the moated manor house of Bartholomew Gosnold's uncle, the likely meeting place where Gosnold, Edward Maria Wingfield, Captain Christopher Newport, Captain John Smith, and Richard Hakluyt planned the Jamestown voyage and settlement . The meeting room fireplace (right), with Otley Hall owner, Nicholas Hagger (left), and author (right).

among his East Anglian friends, neighbors and relatives. He must have been a particularly effective promoter as he, like few others, could tell first-hand of what the Atlantic voyage would be all about and describe "Virginia". It was Gosnold who was the admiral of the 1602 Cuttyhunk colony near Cape Cod. Despite the fact that the colony only lasted a month, it is almost certain that Gosnold would have been able to assure his listeners that the new Virginia adventure would be different. He had learned from the Northumberland (New England) shortcomings and successes, and he could say with conviction that the south of Virginia, he may have argued, was a paradise in comparison to the northern latitudes.[18]

John Smith does credit Gosnold with being the principle promoter of the Virginia venture.[19] Born in 1571 near Ipswich, Suffolk, Gosnold, with his brother Anthony and sisters Elizabeth and Margaret, attended school at his uncle John's moated manor, Otley Hall, the site of future Virginia colony planning sessions. His uncle became secretary to Robert Devereux, the 2nd Earl of Essex, and it was through this family connection that Gosnold became a daring mariner, venturing to the Azores in 1597, and privateering against the Spanish where he accumulated a sizable prize. Essex next intended to fund a New World voyage to include Gosnold, but the Earl's implication in the 1601 Essex Rebellion and his ultimate execution left Gosnold no support for the trip. It was not until the following year that the Earl of Southampton, Wingfield's cousin, stepped forward to fund the Cuttyhunk colony. But despite that rather limited attempt at colonization, Gosnold became known as an outstanding mariner and immediately began planning the attempt to sail to the southern coast of America. By 1605, the plans for a southern colony led by Gosnold were much advanced and by then included Wingfield, Gosnold's cousin, and Gosnold's traveler-soldier friend, Smith. In on the planning as well was Richard Hakluyt, the Younger, the nearby vicar of All Saints Church at Weatheringsett, and the King's official geographer. It was Hakluyt who put into print the most vivid accounts of the English explorations in the New World and the most forceful and convincing arguments for founding English colonies. Otley Hall seems to have been used as the forum for the planning meetings of these promoter/friends and as a base for recruiting men from the vicinity. Judging from the way the East Anglian hometowns cluster on the map of southeastern England, it is logical to assume that Gosnold was an accomplished recruiter for the Virginia venture from the environs of Otley.

When the fleet sailed, however, Christopher Newport became the commanding Admiral and Wingfield, a chief stockholder in the Virginia Company, an aspiring Governor. It was the experienced mariner but second in command, Gosnold, who had to watch helplessly by as the fleet floundered in the mouth of the Thames for almost the entire first month of the voyage. Gosnold also must have been frustrated enduring Newport's long southern route to Virginia via the Canary and West Indian Islands, when he already knew the benefit of the faster northern route. It was, in fact, at their first stop in the Canary Islands that Gosnold's friends, John Smith, Stephen Calthrope, and apparently a John Robinson, were impli-

Figure 8. Vicarage and All Saints Church, Weatheringsett, Suffolk where the vicar, Richard Hakluyt, wrote the reason for and beginnings of a future British colonial empire.

cated in a mutiny. Smith was "restrained," probably in chains, and by the time the fleet got to Nevis in the West Indies, Newport ordered gallows to be constructed to hang him. The hanging never happened, possibly because of the intervention of Gosnold.

We pick up the Jamestown story again in Virginia. Unfortunately the talented Gosnold died, after lingering for a month, at Jamestown on August 22, 1607. He was buried in or near James Fort with full military honors.[20] According to Smith, by December of 1607, 67 of the original 108 settlers had died, and George Percy recorded the deaths of 24 Gentlemen and 1 laborer and 2 others during the months of August and September 1607.[21] The greatest number of the gentlemen from one particular area in England reported by Percy as having died came from London, 11 of 16.[22] Those that died the rest of the summer had come to Virginia from just about every other region in England. It is perhaps significant, however, that the men Captain John Smith took with him during his two voyages of discovery that summer, one to the falls of the James and the other into the Chesapeake, included the men and boys from his home area of Lincolnshire and Norfolk. These adventurers were apparently among those who survived through the summer, or at least George Percy did not add them to his death list. Of course, they were away from Jamestown Island during the real heat of the summer, sailing on the open water which gives more credence to the assumption that Jamestown Island, with its marshes and no fresh spring water, caused the demise of so many so fast. On the other hand, perhaps Smith chose the strongest and healthiest of the group to go with him, thus culling out the people who could have survived anyway had they stayed at the Fort.

In January and April of 1608, two supply ships, the *Phoenix* and the *John and Francis*, arrived with 120 more men. Their biographies and demographics are a subject for future research.

Chapter 2

Discoveries 1999

From the outset, the overall goal of the *Jamestown Rediscovery* excavations was to locate and uncover any remains of the first Jamestown settlement, especially traces of James Fort as it was originally constructed and any other phases that it may have evolved into during the Virginia Company years, 1607-1624.[23] At that time it was the opinion of various visitors to Jamestown Island, beginning as early at 1842 and archaeologists testing the APVA property, that all traces of the James Fort settlement had been victim of James River shoreline erosion.[24] But it is clear from the first five seasons of digging that the archaeological remains of the early settlement escaped erosion. APVA *Jamestown Rediscovery* excavations un-

Figure 9. Jamestown Rediscovery site, 1999.

Figure 10. 1999 Jamestown Rediscovery site overview.

covered the southeastern corner of the fort, 1994-1999.[25] That footprint consisted of slot trenches where upright side-by side log palisades and a curved dry moat once stood. Other signs included two "pits" or cellars inside the palisade lines, one near the southeast corner and another amid the curve of the Fort's corner bulwark, possibly a secondary powder magazine. Both these and the fort moat had been filled in with mixed clay transported there from some other original colonial excavation, as well as rich deposits of discarded armor, pottery, copper, waste from making glass, and garbage bones from the period 1607-1610. Two graves were also uncovered: the burials of a European man and woman. The man, who was the victim of a massive gunshot wound to his lower leg died, between the age of 17-25; the woman in her late thirties. Both were buried in coffins and may have died during the early years of the settlement. Ballistic tests indicated that the scatter of lead shot in the man's wound could not have produced that pattern if he accidentally shot himself from close range. Therefore he was killed by friendly fire or deliberately by someone else. Recent scientific analysis of bone has raised questions about his country of origin and consequently date of death. One test for carbon isotopes suggested he was either native born or from some country other than England, and therefore could not have been among the number of men who died in the summer of 1607.[26] However, another test for lead, strontium, and oxygen isotopes strongly suggests he grew up in the United Kingdom, probably in the southwest of England or Wales.[27] The hexagonal shape of his coffin, a type believed by some to date no earlier than 1650, also suggests that he died much later than 1607.[28] However, the woman buried immediately adjacent to the man was buried in a triangular, gable-lidded coffin, a type common to the early 17th century. The women's carbon isotopic bone tests also indicated she was an immigrant.[29] The research on these two skeletons continues.

During the past two seasons, excavations focused on an L-shaped pit located at the end of a 50-foot palisade wall trench extending east of the east wall of the triangular fort. The total excavation of that feature discovered that the pit was, in fact, a cellar built in two phases under a superstructure supported by fairly regularly spaced upright posts. The palisade attached to the building at what appeared to have been the original southwest corner post of the building, but at some point the cellar was enlarged, apparently by digging beneath the superstructure to form its L-shape. The cellar had a series of entrance steps descending from the west and fanning toward the south so that the room could be entered from the north. It was clear that the cellar once had a timber lining on the east and north walls. There, regular deposits of a different type of fill than the trash and redeposited clay/topsoil defined where the timbers for the walls once lay. The wall on the east held back a mixed clay "liner," presumably packed in there behind the timber to waterproof the wall closest to the actual wall line of the superstructure above. The west wall did not need the waterproofing as it was well under and away from the western outside wall line. By the same token, the original south wall would also not require water-proofing clay as it too was well beneath the superstructure.

The cellar floor was made up of natural subsoil clay in the L-addition, but a mixture of sandy clay leveled the floor in the north half of the structure. In that section, the flooring fill contained a barrel buried upright in the northeast corner of the room. The barrel apparently served as a sump whenever the cellar took on water, which happened on many occasions judging from the lower few inches of washed sand on the floor and the washed sand in the barrel. No barrel wood survived, but the dark stain

Figure 11. Blockhouse (or watchtower?) cellar showing timber postholes partially excavated and stairs (upper right).

Figure 12. Blockhouse (or watchtower?) cellar showing impression of 1) east timber wall, 2) barrel sump, and 3) fire area.

left where the wood decayed formed a perfect mold in the sandy fill around and in it. The washed layers and the installation of the barrel also suggested that the cellar was in use for some length of time.

There was also evidence of a fire along the west wall. Clay, turned red by heat, and charcoal on the floor clearly pinpoint a fire "place." It was not clear if this was a domestic heating or a cooking hearth or both. There was no evidence along the clay cellar wall above the fire area that there had ever been a flue.

Small postholes were found in a line cutting into the subsoil below the floor-leveling fill south of the stairs, suggesting that some sort of a partition existed there before the floor level was raised. A wall there does not make much sense unless there was need, as in a prison, to secure the cellar space from access by the stairs. In fact, there is some reason to believe that the room was used as a dungeon. John Smith tells of putting one of two Powhatan brothers in a "dungeon" until the other brother returned a stolen pistol by sunup.[30] Failure to comply would result in the execution of the prisoner. That night, taking pity on his prisoner, Smith allowed him to burn a charcoal fire. The flueless fire rendered the prisoner unconscious by the time the brother returned the pistol. Thinking him dead, the brother loudly and justifiably cried foul, at which time Smith told the conscious man that if he promised to end forever the arms thievery, he would bring his brother back to life. A stiff shot of alcohol did the trick and, according to Smith, he thereafter had little trouble with getting his way with the Indians. He had the power, so they thought, to raise the dead.

A flueless charcoal fire, perhaps only burned once, and the inner security wall at the base of the steps in the cellar seem to make sense in light of Smith's dun-

Figure 13. Woodcut from Captain John Smith's The Generale Historie depicting the capture of the "King of the Pamarukes." Later a pistol theft by the Powhatan brothers caused an incident involving a dungeon, a likely use of the blockhouse/watchtower cellar.

geon account. But jail or not, it is clear that the cellar did serve as part of the Jamestown defense system. Shelves cut into the north and south walls could have been built there to serve musketeers, thus giving an elevated firing position through a ground-level opening. This makes all the more sense when it appears that the cellar and its superstructure extend so far beyond the palisade wall that it could act as a bastion. In that case, a musketeer could provide flanking fire toward anyone assaulting the palisade.

What the superstructure looked like is difficult to determine from the mere footprint in the clay. However, one thing seems certain—there was more than just a ground level A-frame over the cellar. The fact that the palisade ended with a structural building post assures that the superstructure had to have some considerable elevation to be effective against attack, a minimum of 8-10' high. It is not beyond the realm of possibility either that the building had a second story, taking on the elevation of the "watchtower(s)" that William Strachey mentioned were located at the "corners" of the fort in 1610.[31] It is also possible that the second story was "jettied" beyond the lower story wall, a common practice in town house construction during the 14th–16th centuries in England. The jetty would also serve as a barrier to any attacker attempting to scale the wall.

Figure 14. Site map depicting a hypothetical reconstruction of James Fort palisades and structures uncovered 1994-1999.

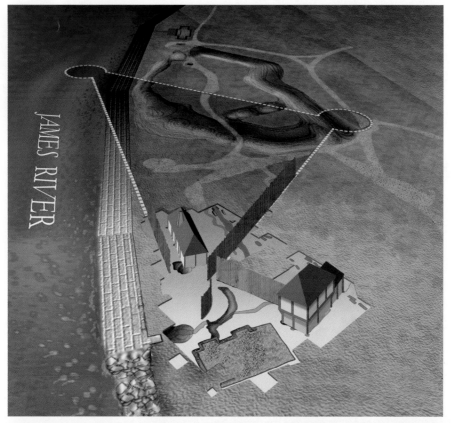

JAMES RIVER

Figure 15. Blockhouse (or watchtower?) cellar showing the half-excavated (1) construction fill under (2) domestic garbage and tras

The cellar held four distinct types of fill laid in there in this sequence: washed sandy clay at the bottom; above that the aforementioned fill that washed in along the floor from the south and on into the barrel sump; next, a major dumping of mixed subsoil and topsoil below a thick vein of trash and garbage spilling in from the south and east; and finally on top, brown loam eventually leveled the resulting depression presumably so that the abandoned fort building site could easily be plowed. The top three layers represent the end of the life of the cellar: the lower mixed clay, the trash and garbage, and the leveling loam. The open cellar itself, before it became a pit to fill in, actually stood under a timber superstructure far larger than just its subterranean undercroft. A number of regularly spaced postholes extend north of the cellar clearly indicating that the building with the cellar was the southernmost section of a much larger building. The postholes show the outline of a room extended to the north of the cellar section, and beyond that a third room with a brick fireplace foundation in the southwestern corner and perhaps another cellar. The brick hearth in the northernmost section shows evidence that it was rebuilt once and that the fire got hot enough to melt some of the floor and firebox bricks. There is also a narrow and shallow trench extending along the connected footings from near the extended palisade to the brick hearth. This may be the bottom of a trench created by water dripping from the roof. In that case, the roof appears to have been a continuous A-form, except perhaps for the southern end of the superstructure. The trench may also be the bottom of a palisade and as such has nothing to do with the form of the roof. In that case perhaps the roof was a series of connected east-west running gables, construction consistent with the type of gabled structures shown on the Vingboons 1617 map at Jamestown and Charles Fort.

Excavations in 1999 were not able to trace the full extent of the extended building. In the coming seasons trenches to the north will extend in that area, but churchyard graves will be a major problem there. Twenty-two were uncovered along the south boundary of the churchyard cemetery. Therefore the digging of the grave shafts throughout the 150-year life of the nearby church resulted in the massive disturbance of the earlier fort related features. However, it still may be possible to trace evidence of the fort between graves.

The layout of the cellar building suggests that another feature of the Fort, actually discovered during the first two seasons of excavation, might have been a similar or identical post-supported building with a cellar. During the second excavation season, eight similar and aligned postholes clearly marked where a rectangular building once stood nine feet from the southeast palisade. Nearby and aligned with the postholes, the first season of excavation uncovered a series

Figure 16. Brick fireplace found in a room to the north of the blockhouse (or watchtower ?) cellar.

of intersecting pits, the earliest being very rectangular. Also a line of postholes led from the post structure to and along the line of the rectangular pit. Further digging north of that posthole line in 1999 determined that the posthole line was not the south wall of a building located more toward the interior of the fort, as we had thought. Rather the wall line had to belong to the posthole complex already uncovered, possibly defining a much longer structure than we earlier recognized. Then, in light of finding the aforementioned "long house" in the fort in 1999, it became rather obvious that we had actually unknowingly found an almost iden-

Figure 17. Enlargements of the houses (?) depicted on a ca. 1617 Dutch chart of the James River, (left to right) "Blockhouse Jamestown" and "Charles Fort," 1617.

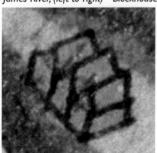

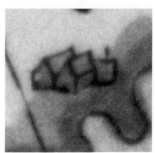

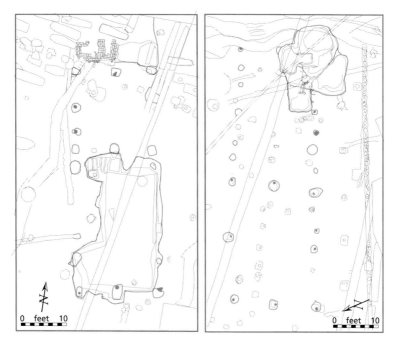

Figure 18. Plan of almost identical post long houses at James Fort, (right) interior of triangular palisade, (left) Blockhouse (or watchtower ?) structure.

tical building outline in earlier seasons. In fact, the posthole patterns of the two series are almost identical. That being the case, it seems logical that the original aligned pit is also a cellar. But this cellar held fill containing clay mixed with cut marsh reeds—a formula that must have been used to make daub material for the walls of houses. The recovery of the daubing originally suggested that the pit was dug to gather clay, then served as a place to mix clay and reeds to finish the walls of a separate house standing on the neat collection of postholes found in the earlier season.

Figure 19. Overview of Fort long house during earlier excavations (1995).

Figure 20. Overhead view of cellar/clay pit at east end of Fort long house.

That now appears to be a secondary use of what started out as a cellar to a much larger building. The rest of the cellar fill was almost identical with the fort extension building cellar fill—lower levels consisting of clay mixed with subsoil coming from another excavation somewhere and garbage and trash from the 1607-1610 period. In fact, several fragments of the same ceramic vessels mended together from cellar to cellar, suggesting that they were abandoned and filled in at the same time, post 1610. The fill in the rectangular pit that proved to be the earliest had an identical sequence of fill: an occupation layer on a leveled floor, below mixed clay, below a more organic fill containing military type artifacts and a tobacco pipe bowl dating to the period 1607-1610. However, when this "cellar" was completely filled in, an unmortared brick foundation, probably used for a crude fireplace, was laid on the backfilled space. This sug-

Figure 21. Archaeologists Danny Schmidt, Eric Deetz, and Seth Mallios marvel at the recovery of a distiller's "boiler jar" (cucurbit) from amid the 1610 artifact assemblage from the blockhouse (or watchtower ?) cellar. It is likely that this jar was used with the glass "condenser" or alembic being discovered below.

gests that the structure remained in use for some extended period of time during which deeper sub-pits came into use. The deepest or last pit, in fact, fits precisely in the southwest corner of the projected superstructure.

It has been noted in previous publications that the interior pit series, the fort moat, the circular pit in the bulwark, and the fill in the exterior cellar were apparently all filled at one time. A convincing number of pieces of the same ceramic vessels fit together from the four sources. The nature of the four deposits were also almost identical: scrap copper, jettons, armor, weapon parts, food remains, and layers of mixed clay without artifacts. Also the most recent artifacts in all the features dated to no later than 1610, therefore all four features seemed to have a similar backfilling date. So because of the nature of the fill and the same back-filling date, it was tempting to ascribe the cultural levels to the massive clean-up ordered by Governor De La Warre upon his arrival with the men and supplies that saved the colony from abandonment in June of 1610[32]. However, it should be noted that the date of the deposits can only be said to date *after* 1610, not necessarily *in* 1610.

Even with De La Warre's reported commitment to revitalizing the fort, it is difficult to explain why *all* of the major subsurface footprints of the fort buildings and moat would be abandoned, presumably during other construction. This is especially so since the chronicler, William Strachey, describes the fort so precisely as still triangular in form as Percy and Smith did, even though it was, as he said, "lately brought to perfection" presumably by the efforts of De La Warre's men. Strachey held that the fort was a triangular shape with two 300' sides on the north and a 420' side on the south made of "planks and strong posts."[33] Perhaps the explanation lies in Strachey's earlier description of the town, written about what he saw on May 20, 1610, when he arrived with the previously shipwrecked party from Bermuda. He makes a strong point that the town was in shambles with the main gate off the hinges and the houses and palisade torn down and cut into firewood.[34] It is significant that previous excavations indicated that the east wall of the fort was purposely removed, possibly as a result of this desperate gathering of firewood.[35] Of course the removal left the whole settlement wide open to attacks from the Powhatan, unless the east palisade had become an interior wall, rendered obsolete by the "five-sided" fort built after the 1608 fire.[36] In any case, if an exterior wall was down then it is understandable that, as Strachey remarked, the Indians would kill anyone who ventured from their 'blockhouse,' the only protected place left in which to hide out.[37] The "blockhouse" could mean, of course, that the survivors were confined to the blockhouse that had been built near the isthmus at the extreme western end of the island or the blockhouse on Back River. But it is also possible that the settlers were seeking safety in the cellar building or buildings in the fort which had become, in a sense, a blockhouse or fort house when the palisades were

Figure 22. 1610 John Speed map of Shrowesbury showing contiguous town houses, some forming part of a defensive town wall.

gone. Strachey also remarked that they were suffering from pestilence from within the blockhouse. If they were in fact trapped inside the buildings for their own safety, then it is not beyond the realm of possibility that their garbage and trash could wind up in the cellar, below them. Under siege by the Indians, who would risk an appearance beyond the protection of the blockhouse walls just to get rid of rubbish? While that might explain the garbage and some of the trash in the cellars it does not account for the industrial waste: from glassmaking, pipemaking, metallurgy, and reworking armor, nor does it explain the essentially artifact-free clay

Figure 23. 1608 Map of Fort St. George , the Plymouth Company's 1607-08 settlement in Maine. Recent excavations by archaeologist Jeffrey P. Brain are verifying that the map accurately depicts long post buildings, apparently not unlike contemporary Jamestown structures.

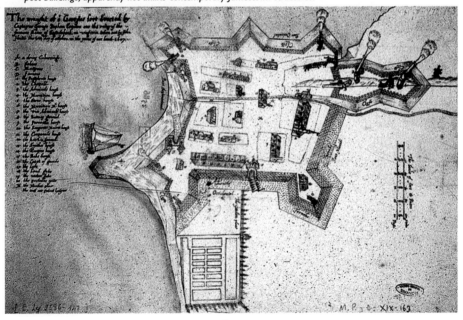

Figure 24. Except for the contiguous sections of the storehouse (lower right), current excavations are suggesting that the "skyline" of James Fort and adjacent areas was considerably different than this 1957 artist's view based only on documentary descriptions.

in the lowest levels of each cellar. The starving, trapped settlers would hardly bide their time by busily manufacturing things and dumping the industrial waste in the cellar below. Nor could they dig new holes elsewhere beyond the security of the blockhouse walls and bring the spoil back for disposal in the cellar either. Indeed, the redeposited clay layer must have gone into the cellar hole after the superstructure no longer stood. So it seems then that the blockhouse confinement brought on by the Indian siege is not a convincing explanation for the cellar garbage. What is left is the possibility that the filled-in sites were abandoned in favor of freshly trenched earthworks or dug cellars somewhere else nearby, perhaps part of an improved fortification. If that is true, then a newer version of the fort will likely be uncovered as the excavations expand.

In any case, besides the church, there is only one reference to measurements of any long structure during the early years at Jamestown. In 1611 Ralph Hamor describes the storehouse as such a building, 120 feet in length[38] He also mentions two streets of houses two stories and a loft high. In 1952 artist Sydney King considered all the descriptions of James Fort/ James Towne, and being as true to the evidence as he could, painted two bird's-eye views of the two periods of the town. With the exception of the long storehouse, he pictures either minute, single, stand-alone "cabins" or larger stand-alone houses in the expanded townsite. The recent archaeological evidence of long houses, obviously not known to King, casts considerable doubt on his view of the single cabins and perhaps even the later houses. In fact, the King houses would be at odds with what the settlers left in their towns in England and what the Plymouth Company settlers built at St. George's Fort in Maine in 1607.

Figure 25. Discarded animal and fish remains from the cellar of the fort long house—remnants of the 1609-1610 "starving time?"

Starving Time

The considerable quantity of animal bones, the remains of the meat people were eating, found in the pits on the interior of the fort have been identified. This collection of bones gives vivid testimony to hard life at Jamestown during those first precarious years, 1607-ca.1610.[39] That date for the deposit can be fairly precisely determined owing to the number of objects datable stylistically or historically and the number of dated coins recovered.[40] Actually some of the bones turned out to be the most precisely datable evidence of the collection. How so? Strachey reported that he and the shipwrecked Bermuda contingent arrived at Jamestown in May 1610 with provisions that were collected during their shipbuilding stay in Bermuda.[41] The cellar held the bones of birds, especially the petrel, which could only be found in Bermuda, as well as Bermudan conches and a number of tropical fish common to those islands. Some pieces of Bermudan limestone were also found in this cellar fill. There is no other record from any other time of supplies coming into Virginia from Bermuda. It follows then that these uniquely Bermudan food supplies were brought to Jamestown in May 1610 by the ex-*Sea Venture* passengers, eaten by them and the survivors of the Starving Time at Jamestown, after which they discarded the bones in the fort cellar.[42]

It also appears that the voyagers were not carrying great quantities of extra supplies on their trip from Bermuda to Jamestown, as they had no way of knowing that they would find a starving Jamestown. Upon landing Sir Thomas Gates took over leadership from George Percy and immediately saw the urgent need to realistically assess the ratio of population to his provisions. He concluded, at first, that the Bermudan food supplies would be kept in reserve for a possible retreat voyage back to England while he, in the meantime, would send parties out to forage among the Powhatan, hopefully to gather enough food to get the colony back on its feet. Having no luck there, he figured that at that point there was enough food for the colonists to survive at Jamestown for 16 days, if he rationed two cakes (possibly a type of dried fish cake) per person per day.[43] If no supplies could be found during that two plus weeks period, they would abandon the colony. No food materialized. They would have to leave. On June 6, the settlers buried the ordinance and whatever else they had hopes of reclaiming if they ever came back. Then with everything else of value, they headed downriver toward the open ocean. The group intended to spend time on the Grand Banks fishing grounds off Newfoundland to replenish their food supplies. However, they also planned to stop at the Charles and Algernon Fort area and wait two weeks for possible English supplies to arrive.[44] There, for the short term, they knew they could live off shellfish like the healthy party of original settlers who greeted them on their way in from Bermuda. After being away from Jamestown for just over a day, the arrival of an advance boat brought the announcement of the imminent arrival of the new governor, Lord De La Warre, with enough new men and supplies to save the day.[45]

Besides dating the collection with evidence of the Bermudan provisions, the discarded food bones from the fort cellar graphically underscore just how serious the Starving Time was for those who tried to hold the fort during the winter and spring of 1609-1610. The presence of poisonous snake vertebrate, musk turtle, and raptors give some indication that life at Jamestown had reached crisis proportions. Moreever butchered horse bones and the bones of the black rat, dogs, and cats powerfully demonstrate how dire the condition of the colonists had become. For example, fifteen bones or bone fragments of a large dog or dogs were recovered from the fill in the dry moat of the southeast bulwark. These did not show signs of butchering but, being with the other bones that did may indicate that while these animals were brought to Virginia as hunters or "weapons" of

Figure 26. Horse's hoof (left) and poisonous snake vertebrae from "food" remains deposits.

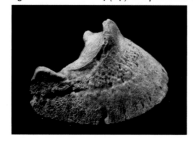 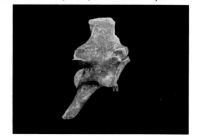

war, they did eventually become a food source. It is significant too that x-rays of skull fragments found show that dogs at Jamestown lived hard lives even before they wound up on the dinner table. The radiograph shows a small piece of lead shot imbedded in the skull. This was not, however, the cause of death as the x-ray also showed that the bone had

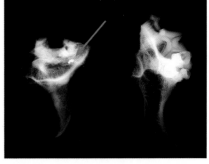

Figure 27. X-ray of dog skull fragments showing lead shot healed in place.

healed around the shot. It seems logical to assume that the injury came from combat after the Powhatan acquired muskets—as early as 1608 according to John Smith.[46] Documentary sources indicate clearly that the Indians realized the strategic importance of the colonists' dogs, even before they used muskets. Gabriel Archer reported as early as May 1607, that while the settlers themselves escaped harm, one Powhatan attack on the Jamestown settlers resulted in the killing of "our dogs." Of course the Indians may have had nothing to do with the shot in the skull of the once wounded dog. It is likely that the lead wound up there as the result of a stray hunting shot. In any case, here is another sign of extreme hunger; the starving colonists resorted to killing and eating one of the very key means they had to more easily live off the wilderness. Of course, if the settlers were confined to their "blockhouse" as Strachey reports, then domesticates like dogs and cats and anything else living "inside" like rats would become the only source of food for the besieged colonists. So Percy apparently is not exaggerating when he wrote that during that Starving Time, "Then having fed upon horses and other beasts as long as they lasted, we were glad to make shift with vermin, as dogs, cats, rats and mice."[47]

Figure 28. Detail from John Smith's Map of Virginia showing Susquehanna Indian with what appears to be a native dog on his back.

The exact specie of the lead-carrying dog is not precisely known, but it has characteristics of a mastiff.[48] There is no question that it was relatively large, perhaps in the 45-55 pound range. According to records, greyhounds and mastiffs were at Jamestown, and perhaps this skull comes from one of those. Chances

The Sasque- ahanougs are a Gyant like peo= ple & thus a tyred

are this is not the skull of a Native American dog. A rendering of one American dog suggests that they were relatively small with very distinctive skull shapes. Some believe that relatives of these Indian dogs still roam free in the backwoods of coastal North Carolina.[49]

In any case, things were so bad that Strachey reports that only 60 survived of the 500 people at Jamestown during this Starving Time.[50] A combination of numbers from several eyewitness accounts, however, suggests that while the death rate at Jamestown was apalling, it has been exaggerated. By adding and subtracting population estimates with accounts of individual and group deaths, and numbers arriving on various ships, one can estimate that by the fall of 1609, the beginning of the Starving Time, there were 215 people at Jamestown and 30 living elsewhere. By the arrival of the group from Bermuda then, there were 90 left alive in the colony with 60 in the town. So the survival rate was not 1 in 9 but rather around 1 in 3. But with the influx of the estimated 135 *Sea Venture* survivors, the totals at Jamestown jumped to 195. No wonder they quickly ran out of food and had no choice but to leave. The arrival of the De La Warre entourage could have swelled the Jamestown population to 345. So if De La Warre actually brought provisions to support the total population for a year as reported, then his ships must have been heavy laden indeed.[51]

Church Graveyard

Grave shaft outlines were not only found in the vicinity of the brick hearth of the fort extension long house but also along the entire southern edge of the churchyard, as one might expect. A smaller group of four graves was found to the west and two large rectangular graves in between. The cluster of 22 on the east was oriented almost perfectly east-west, and therefore seem to be part of the churchyard cemetery used during the lifetime of the various churches. It is logical to assume that most of the burials date before about the mid-18th century when the church congregation moved to the mainland. Soon after it was abandoned, the brick church of ca.1639 fell into ruins, then it was dismantled. Some of the bricks were salvaged to build a wall enclosing a small area of marked graves.[52]

None of the graves were excavated below the subsoil level except near the long house brick hearth. There, an attempt was made to excavate a burial shaft deep enough to determine the nature of what appeared to be another cellar in the building, without going deep enough to disturb bone. However, at a depth of only a few inches below the plowzone, coffin nails were found in place indicating that bone would not be much deeper. Excavation was temporarily halted.

The four rather isolated burials on the west seemed to be part of another, perhaps earlier, cemetery and possibly related in time to the man who was shot and the woman found 40' to the south in 1996 (see p. 12). They all seemed to be part of the same burial ground, not only because

Figure 29. Burial JR316 of a Caucasian man who died past age 50, buried in a hexagonal coffin and apparently in clothing with mid-eighteenth century buttons.

they were relatively close by, but also because they were on roughly the same orientation, fairly far south of a true east-west alignment. Intersecting soil layers also suggested that these western graves were very old. A ditch thought to possibly be from the James Fort period cut through and therefore postdated the shaft fill of one of the burials. Excavation proved that two of the burial shafts were extremely deep, and both burials turned out to have been placed in hexagonal coffins. The fill in both shafts was almost devoid of artifacts or contained artifacts from the James Fort period, raising expectations that they could well date to the first few months of the settlement. However, one grave held a skeleton of an adult Caucasian male buried in clothing with five buttons.[53] This type of button was not made any earlier than about 1750, therefore this burial post-dated the 1607 settlement by at least a century and a half. A mid-18th-century bottle also turned up in the fill of the "fort" ditch after the buttons were recovered, so the fact that the ditch covered one of the burials did not mean it was actually an early grave after all. The other excavated burial was of a Caucasian woman in her twenties buried in a shroud held together by at least four brass pins. No artifacts were found to determine when during the colonial period she was buried. Both were on the same orientation and at identical depths so may well be contemporary—18th century.

Excavations in the 2000 season will continue to explore Jamestown burials but will not concentrate on the churchyard. Another cemetery, located on the extreme western end of the APVA property beneath the foundations of the traditional site of the late-17th-century "Statehouse," will be systematically examined. There is reason to believe that this cemetery

Figure 30. Foundations of the Ludwell Statehouse complex: contiguous building footings and cellars of a structure that included a section of "the statehouse" in 1694. It is located on the western edge of the APVA Jamestown property.

holds burials from the Starving Time. These and the later building foundations will almost certainly reveal new evidence of these significant chapters of the Jamestown story for future site interpretation.

In 1694 a patent granted the land and ruins of three houses located between the "statehouse" and the "country house" to Philip Ludwell.[54] There is no question as to the location of this patent, which is a 1.5 acre lot that lies today within the central part of the massive five part foundation just west of the APVA Yeardley House. The eastern end of this complex served as the "statehouse," and it is likely that the "country house" on the west served some governmental function, as well. The name "country house" meant that it belonged to the "country," or in other words technically, at least, owned by the Colony. In 1698 the statehouse at Jamestown burned and the following year the capital moved to Williamsburg. It is likely that the statehouse that burned in 1698 stood on the APVA foundation, though there is no direct record of where the government meeting building or buildings were at the time of the fire. It appears that buildings were not rebuilt on the foundations of the APVA Statehouse foundations, even though the James City County court still functioned at Jamestown until 1715. There is a reference to the removal of bricks from the statehouse ruin at Jamestown to be used for construction in Williamsburg. There is also clear evidence that some public governmental meetings were held in the APVA Statehouse complex in the mid-1650s, indicating perhaps that the building existed by that date and perhaps as early as 1645.[55] In any case, while the assembly, council, and court were held at other Jamestown buildings at various times, it is clear that the APVA Ludwell-Statehouse complex served a public governmental function.

The next reference of importance to the complex followed an excavation of the foundations by Col. Samuel Yonge in 1903 and recorded in his book *The Site of Old Jamestown*, published in 1907.[56] In it he describes what he found, and he published a photo of one of the cellars and a drawing of the foundation he uncovered. It is important to note that from what he found he concluded that the building burned and that the eastern section of what appeared to be a five-part building could well match the description of the governmental functions of various spaces recorded in a

Figure 31. Photo and plan of 1903 Statehouse excavations by Colonel Samuel Yonge.

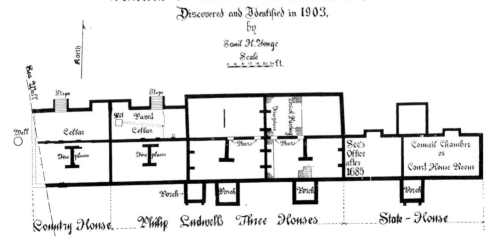

document signed by "T.M" in 1694.[57] While the excavation was crude by modern standards, this work and Yonge's study of erosion and other patents at Jamestown were remarkably thorough and insightful. For example, he was one of the few who thought remains of James Fort still could be found on land in the vicinity of the church tower. That, of course, proved to be true. In any event it appeared that his excavation cleared away the debris from the fire (of 1698 or even from the 1676 Bacon's Rebellion burning?) leaving no real detailed record of either building materials or dates of events. The importance of such artifacts was not recognized at the time. In any event, the foundations were capped with reinforced concrete, fenced in with a wrought iron fence, still in place today, and left exposed above ground for interpretation.

In the early 1950s, the APVA and the National Park Service seriously considered reconstruction of the statehouse section of the foundation complex for the 350th celebration of Jamestown's founding. This plan led to two NPS archaeological investigations of the eastern foundation. Archaeologist Louis Caywood led the first excavation in 1954. He basically dug along the exposed eastern end of the foundations, opening trenches three feet on either side of the brickwork. He found evidence of a partition wall undetected by Yonge, burned floor joists, some roofing tiles and slate, and he recovered bones from six graves. NPS archaeologist, Joel Shiner, took over the excavations the following year to explore the cemetery component of the site. He cleared away all of the topsoil and whatever accumulated building debris Caywood missed down to the top of pre-building subsoil, in order to locate and test these additional graves. Shiner found 70 grave outlines and uncovered the bones from seven. Both Caywood and Shiner concluded that the graves predated the building of the Statehouse group, probably by enough years to have erased all memory of the unmarked burial ground. They concluded that the sometimes helter-skelter orientation of many of the graves might indicate that they were from the 1609-10 winter of the Starving Time.

The NPS excavated a total of 17 statehouse graves. While these excavations occurred over 42 years ago, the condition of the bone at that time suggests that excavation of a representative sample today will recover enough skeletal material for conservation and substantial analysis. The recovery of a statistically valid sample of the burials could learn much about the individuals: gender, social status, age at death, their diet, whether foreign or native born, their general health, signs of some diseases, possibly cause of death, their burial ritual, and the date after which the burial occurred. The study could also determine ratio of men, women, and children, possible family relationships, life expectancy, and disease or trauma patterns in the general Jamestown population.

Figure 32. Hypothetical reconstruction on its Jamestown site of the likely 2nd quarter 17th-century Ludwell/Statehouse complex façade, using the 16th-century timber-framed Guildhall in Lavenham, England and Virginia's 1665 Bacon's Castle as templates.

Figure 33. Diagram showing information that can be learned from skeletal remains.

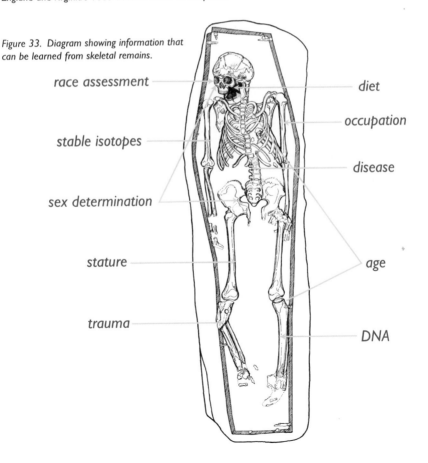

race assessment

diet

occupation

stable isotopes

disease

sex determination

stature

age

trauma

DNA

Conclusion

The *Jamestown Rediscovery* research team completed the first half of its ten-year plan by finding and beginning to uncover the form of James Fort and its evolving architectural history during its earliest years. Documentary research, while in its infancy, is beginning to give biographies to the mostly heretofore anonymous faces of the original settlers. Hopefully continued genealogical work will give more substance to the biographies of those first adventurers and for those delivered with the supply ships that soon followed. Archaeology has also clarified how these early Jamestown founders adapted their settlement more to the realities of Virginia as time passed and how they survived despite the horrendous Starving Time. The multitude of artifacts recovered during the course of the excavations also reflects a hard working colony—one that stands in stark contrast to the story that blames Jamestown hardships and near failure on its lazy gentlemen. With only an estimated 15 percent of the early Jamestown site uncovered in these first six years, there can be no doubt that by the 400th anniversary of Jametown's founding in 2007, future *Jamestown Rediscovery* research will uncover and give even more meaning to the long buried remnants of the first enduring settlement of the English in America.

Chapter 3

by Beverly Straube

Tinker, tailor, soldier, sailor …

Of all the surviving documents relating to the early English coloniz-ing effort at Jamestown, it appears that the backward lens of history has crystallized around a single remark. In 1615, colonist Ralph Hamor re-lates that when Thomas Dale arrived at Jamestown, "where the most company were," in May 1611, he found the men at "their daily and usuall works bowling in the streets."[58] The picture engendered by this statement, of men engaged in idle entertainment while their dilapidated houses were ready to fall upon their heads, has come down through history to epito-mize the early colonizing efforts at Jamestown. The perception has been that the first individuals sent to Jamestown were a bunch of bumbling idiots who didn't know what they were doing, refused to work, and chose the worst possible place to settle on low, swampy, unhealthy ground that almost spelled the demise of the colony. Jamestown as a joke, a settlement that nearly failed, is not a very noble representation for the beginnings of America, as we know it today. Perhaps this is why historians have largely ignored Jamestown, and when patriotism stirs Americans to remember their roots, thoughts are of Plymouth, a successful colony based on re-spectable religious principles, and not that scruffy military-economic settlement in Virginia.

The *Jamestown Rediscovery* excavations on the site of James Fort are uncovering information that contradicts this characterization of early Jamestown. While it is probably true that many of the colonists who par-ticipated in the Virginia adventure the first few years were "poore Gentle-men, Tradsmen, Serving-men, [and] libertines"[59] and did not contribute much to sustaining the fledgling colony, archaeology is revealing another compelling story. Artifacts in the way of tools, equipment, and industrial byproducts indicate that many of the craftsmen were actively working at what they had been sent to do—trying to make money for the investors at home in England.

During the first one and a half years of colonization at Jamestown al-most 300 individuals arrived for the purpose of turning a profit for the Virginia Company, the London-based group of entrepreneurs who were bankrolling the enterprise. The colonists were not sent with the idea of establishing a new country. Instead, they were to set up a *center of exploi-tation* whereby they could venture out from a secured home base and ex-tract any marketable resources the land had to offer. According to the "instructions by way of advice" that the colonists were given by the gov-erning council of the Virginia Company, they were even expected to pull the Indians into this system of *resource extraction* as the primary suppliers of "corn and all other lasting victuals."[60] The colonists were supposed to

Figure 34. Bowling was a popular leisure-time activity for men and women in all levels of English society, as it required little more than a grassy area or alley and the bowls (balls). Gambling was usually associated with the game, as was rowdy behavior, which often led to prohibitions against bowling on the Sabbath. The men in this Dutch painting are playing skittles, a type of bowling game using nine wooden pins as the target. Skittles is the precursor of the modern bowling game of ten pins.

establish a symbiotic relationship with "the naturals," whereby European trade beads and copper jewelry would be exchanged for foodstuffs to sustain the settlement. "This," instructs the Council for Virginia, "you must do before…they perceive you mean to plant among them."[61] Opening up large areas of land in cultivation right away would send a signal of permanency that might alarm, and possibly alienate, the Indians. Reliance on the "country corn" made sense, not only because it was not known how well the planted English seed would prosper, but also because, ideally, it would help frame a friendly rapport with the native inhabitants whose information on the local resources was needed. Most importantly, it freed the colonists to focus on their principal goal, which was profit for the investors. The men "were not permitted to manure or till any ground" but were directed by the Virginia Company to engage in activities that would "make return of present profit."[62] The low priority farming held for the Jamestown settlers is exemplified by the fact that only two agricultural hoes have been recovered by archaeologists from over 108,000 artifacts in the pre-1610 contexts in James Fort.

Luckily for us, John Smith recorded the names of many of the colonizers—common craftsmen as well as men of position—with the arrival of every supply and at the outset of each expedition. As cape merchant for the colony, he was the officer in charge of supply and would have had lists of all the individuals who had arrived at Jamestown and whom he was responsible to provision.[63] The majority of the men are identified as gentlemen, many of whom were veterans of wars in the Low Countries and/or Ireland, and largely comprised the military component. Others are described generally as laborers or tradesmen, but some are labeled with their specific crafts, many of which seem superfluous to the survival of the colony.

Smith bemoans the Virginia Company's drive for profit at the expense of the settlement's welfare which he claims "most plainly appeared by sending…so many Refiners, Gold-smiths, Jewellers, Lapidaries, Stone-cutter, Tabacco-pipe-makers, Imbroderers, Perfumers, Silkemen with all their appurtenances."[64] None of the colonists on Smith's surviving lists are identified specifically as lapidaries, embroiderers, or silkmen, but the refiners, goldsmiths, a jeweller, a stone-cutter (or mason), a tobacco pipe maker, and a perfumer are named. In addition, several other craftsmen are identified in the records with trades not on Smith's "worthless" list, such as blacksmiths, bricklayers, and carpenters (Appendix). What do we know about these identified craftsmen and what objects have been unearthed that may relate to the practice of their crafts at Jamestown? Most importantly, why were these particular individuals chosen to be among the first to exploit Virginia's resources?

Figure 35. Goldsmiths were of high status in early 17th-century English society. They not only worked with precious metals and stones but also were merchants dealing in these expensive materials.

Refiners and Goldsmiths

Based upon the Spanish experience in the New World, the English also hoped to find riches—particularly gold and silver—in the Virginia soils. The search began almost immediately upon the first landing at Jamestown in May 1607; so, when Christopher Newport returned to London in June he was able to carry what he believed to be samples of gold ore. Unfortunately, when the "gold" was tested by London assayers, "all turned to vapore."[65] But this did not dissuade the effort, especially since Newport claimed that he must have mistakenly brought the wrong sample. The Virginia Company continued to believe in the accuracy of Newport's assessment that Virginia was "very rich in gold and copper."[66] So, on the next ship to the colony, which arrived in January 1608, they sent two refiners (William Dawson and Abram Ransack) and two goldsmiths (William Johnson and Richard Belfield).

Goldsmiths were craftsmen who, as their name suggests, worked with precious metals to fabricate jewelry, drinking and eating vessels, as well as decorative objects. They comprised the wealthiest and most powerful metalworkers in London up to the middle of the 18th century.[67] Since, as we know, gold was not found by the colonists in Virginia, it is not surprising that John Smith tells us that the goldsmiths never had an opportunity to exercise their craft.

The refiners are a different story. Smith had little respect for the "guilded refiners with their golden promises." Dawson and Ransack not only recruited most of the colonists in a frantic search for gold along the muddy banks of the James River, but also detained a shipload of mariners from returning to London in order to do the same. For fourteen weeks "there was no talke, no hope, no worke, but dig gold, wash gold, refine gold, loade gold."[68] The outcome was a depleted store of provisions from the extra burden of supporting the mariners for this length of time. In addition, there was no progress made on the colony's essential duties, and a shipload of "guilded durt" was sent back to London.[69]

Another refiner, William Callicut (Caldicot), probably arrives with the Second Supply in September 1608. He is "fitted" for the purpose of refining, as he accompanies Newport west on an expedition into the territory of the Monacan Indians in October 1608. Smith relates that "from that crust of earth we digged he perswaded us to beleeve he extracted some small quantitie of silver."[70] The assays appeared to confirm silver ore, but, as Smith reveals, the quality was "so poore it was not regarded."[71] This test did not dissuade others from believing Callicut's assessment that "not unlikely better stuffe might be had for the digging." In 1628, a letter to

Figure 36. A still, composed of elements in the same shape and of the same materials as the James Fort still, can be seen sitting by the alchemist's right knee.

the king from the General Assembly at Jamestown refers to Callicut's silver mine discovered "nineteen years ago, at a place about four days' journey from the falls of the James river." The letter goes on to explain that the reason this resource has not been exploited is that there is "not the means of transporting the ore."[72]

Refiners were specialist goldsmiths who refined or separated precious metals. The processes of distillation and cupellation involved in the refiner's work and materials relating to each have been recovered from the site. Cupellation was used in the process of assaying or testing the purity of metals. The sample to be refined was melted with lead, which oxidized forming lead oxide. The lead oxide also oxidized any base metals present in the sample leaving a residue of silver or gold.

A shallow vessel known as a cupel, which was used in small-scale cupellation, was excavated from the site. It is made of bone ash, which was preferred by refiners because this material would absorb the lead oxide leaving a purer residue.[73] The James Fort cupel has some residues indicating that it was used.

Vessels associated with distillation have also been uncovered. Distillation was used in the production of nitric acid, which was required for the

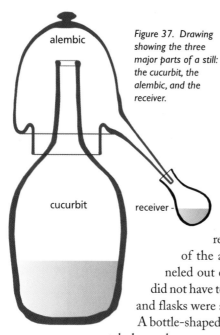

alembic

cucurbit

receiver -

Figure 37. Drawing showing the three major parts of a still: the cucurbit, the alembic, and the receiver.

parting or separation of gold from silver. Metallurgists produced nitric acid by a method known since the 14th century by distilling sulfuric acid with sodium or potassium nitrate.

A distilling unit consists of two main parts: the lower vessel, or cucurbit, and the upper vessel with a spout and domed head known as an alembic. The liquid was boiled in the cucurbit, the resulting vapor condensed within the head of the alembic, and the condensate was channeled out of its spout into a receiver. The receiver did not have to be a specialized vessel. Domestic bottles and flasks were also used to catch the distilled liquid.[74]

A bottle-shaped cucurbit, or distillation flask, with a long tubular neck was recovered from the cellar of Structure 165. It is unglazed and is made of the London red earthenware fabric. Several of these vessels have been recovered from London metalworking contexts dating c.1580-1650.[75] These London vessels exhibit residues of hematite, which is a by-product of the distillation of ferrous sulfate to produce sulfuric acid.[76] The Jamestown flask has no such residue, and therefore was either never used or was used in another distillation process, such as the production of alcohol or perfumes.

Both a glass alembic section, incorporating the complete bottom rim with part of the collection channel, and a fragment of its spout have been found in the same fort context as the flask. Alembics were

Figure 38. Bottom collar section of a glass alembic found in the pre-1610 cellar of Structure 165 (below), and a London earthenware distillation flask from the same context (right).

also made of earthenware fabrics,[77] but it would not be unusual to mix the two materials in the distilling unit. A glass alembic is depicted in use over a distilling flask made of earthenware in Cornelis Bega's painting *The Alchemist*.

Other recovered objects that possibly relate to the distilling efforts of the refiners are distilling dishes, an earthenware dipper, and refractory

Figure 39. Distilling equipment recovered from the excavations include a distilling dish (front left), an earthenware dipper (center), and Hessian crucibles

clay crucibles. The dishes and the dipper are also made of the London redware clay and have been found in association with metalworking in England.[78] The crucibles are of the triangular Hessian type, which were preferred by metalworkers for the fine pouring stream they provided. One crucible contains interior deposits of copper, which could be the result of heating hydrated sulfates of copper to produce sulfuric acid.[79] As previously mentioned, this acid is required to make the nitric acid needed for refining.

Jeweler

A jeweler by the name of Daniel Stallings arrived with the first supply in January 1608. Jewelers in England were variously retailers and appraisers of gemstones and rarely were the craftsmen who actually set the stones.[80] Stallings was probably sent by the Virginia Company to survey the landscape for its potential as a source of gems. At the time, foreign merchants had control of the importation of precious and semiprecious stones into England. Most of the favored stones came from far-off places. Garnets, for instance, came from Bohemia and Sri Lanka.[81]

Stallings may be responsible for the collection of garnets, amethysts, and quartz crystals that have been recovered from the pre-1610 fill of Structure 165. He could have found these materials washing out of the cliffs on the James River beaches or during expeditions up Virginia's waterways.

Figure 40. A collection of semiprecious stones found within the pre-1610 fill of Structure 165.

Figure 41. Masons were buyers and sellers of stone as well as the craftsmen who shaped the stone and built the walls of masonry buildings. They were typically the most highly paid workers on a construction site.

Mason

A mason by the name of Edward Brinton (Brinto/ Brynton) arrived at Jamestown with the initial group of colonists in May 1607. He is probably the "stone-cutter" to whom Smith refers, because masons were specialized craftsmen who were qualified to cut and carve stone for major building projects, as well as to do the initial quarrying. No tools relating to masonry have been excavated from James Fort, but there is further information in the historical records on Brinton's activities while at Jamestown.

Despite John Smith's disparaging remarks about his craft in the aforementioned quote, Brinton must have been respected by Smith, for he was selected by him to be a "soldier" on a December 1608 food gathering expedition to Powhatan's home at Werowocomoco. Brinton also must have been skilled in the use of firearms since he was left "to kill…foule" for Powhatan while the rest of the expedition continued their mission.[82] Smith would not have chosen an inexperienced marksman to hunt for the powerful leader of the Algonquian Indian chiefdom. Firearms, with their fiery retorts and occasional deadly consequences, gave the colonists an advantage in their dealings with the Indians. The latter respected the power of these weapons. It would not be wise, as the Council for Virginia advised, to allow "your learners miss what they aim at" in front of the Indians, for "they will think the weapon not so terrible, and thereby will be bold to assault you."[83]

Most Englishmen at this time were not well trained in the use of firearms. Guns were expensive and hunting preserves were for the wealthy, so the common man would have had nowhere to practice, even if he owned a weapon. Expertise in hunting on the part of a tradesman indicates a certain level of wealth and is reflective, in Brinton's case, of the high status of masons in English society.

Since masons at the time were also stone merchants,[84] Brinton's inclusion with the first group of colonists is totally understandable from a monetary perspective. He was not in the colony to construct masonry buildings. More likely, he was expected to survey the landscape for known and unknown lithic materials that could be successfully marketed in London.

Tobacco Pipemaker

The inclusion of a tobacco pipemaker in the first groups of craftsmen is as enigmatic to researchers today as it apparently was to John Smith when Robert Cotton, "tobacco-pipe-maker," arrived on the *Phoenix* in January 1608.[85] No other mention is made of Cotton, so it is not known how long he remained at Jamestown; although, he is not listed in the

Figure 42. Tobacco pipe with distinctive markings (shown in detail), thought to be the product of Robert Cotton, "tobacco-pipe-maker," who arrived at Jamestown in January 1608.

muster of 1624-25, so presumably he had either perished or returned to England by then. With archival information lacking, the material evidence in the way of very accomplished mold-made clay tobacco pipes, fabricated from the Virginia red clay and decorated on the stem with European stamps, may provide the sole documentation for this early craftsman's work. These distinctive pipes only occur in the early James Fort features dating around 1610 and have not yet been recorded on any other early Virginia sites.

The design of the stamp consists of four fleurs-de-lis forming a cross within a diamond. The sides of the diamond are incurving, as on the 1580-1610 pipes documented in England and thought to be the product of London pipemaker William Batchelor.[86] Robert Cotton must also have been a London pipemaker, because pipemaking was almost entirely restricted to that city by monopoly until the second decade of the 17th century.[87] Other aspects of Cotton's stamp reflect decorative motifs of late-16th- and early-17th-century London pipes which most often include incuse "diamond patterns enclosing initials, crosses or fleur-de-lis on the stems."[88]

Along with the many fragments of Robert Cotton pipes, there have been pieces of what appear to be pipemaking saggars. A saggar is a portable clay container in which the pipes would have been fired to keep them out of direct contact with the flames. This piece of kiln furniture would be particularly necessary if the pipemaker were sharing his furnace with another craftsman. The early craftsmen working within the confines of James Fort probably had to share one source of heat for the production of their wares.

Figure 43. Fragments of a clay saggar probably made by Cotton to fire his clay pipes.

Figure 44. By the late 16th century, smoking had become tremendously popular in English society. English soldiers who were in the Low Countries to fight the Spanish introduced the Dutch to tobacco's pleasures. In this painting by Adrian Brouwer, the artist depicted himself as a mercenary soldier sharing tobacco and a mug of beer with acquaintances in a Dutch tavern.

By the late 16th century, tobacco smoking was a very popular pastime in England among the upper classes. It had been introduced into the country by English explorers to the Americas, such as Sir John Hawkins and Sir Francis Drake, and was first adapted as a medical treatment. As early as 1573, the English are curing ailments by "the taking-in of the smoke of the Indian herbe called 'Tobaco' by an instrument formed like a little ladell."[89] It is not known of what material the "ladell" was made, but, by 1598, tobacco was being smoked in clay pipes. A German lawyer noted in that year that "the English are constantly smoking Tobacco...they have pipes on purpose made of clay."[90]

The white ball clay from Poole, Dorset, on the southern coast of England, was the preferred clay for 17th-century tobacco pipes, and remained so through the 19th century. It fired up white and hard and is called white ball clay, after the practice of forming the mined clay into large balls that could be easily rolled onto wagons for shipment.[91] Lots of English pipe clay was also exported to the Netherlands for their pipemaking industry, supposedly established after 1608 by political refugees from England.[92] Some of these early pipemakers may indeed have been English veterans of the Dutch war of independence from Spain, as were many of the first Virginia colonists.

Pipemaking was a low class trade requiring minimal investment in tools, materials, and training. Pipes were inexpensive but, luckily for the pipemaker, also easily breakable, so pipes were produced and sold in great quantities.

Figure 45. A young soldier uses a candle to light a white ball clay pipe. These small-bowled pipes were made in both England and the Netherlands in the early 17th century.

Why was Robert Cotton at Jamestown? The presence of this craftsman at early Jamestown and the fact that he practiced his craft could indicate how important smoking was to the early colonists, particularly the gentlemen. They knew they were coming to a place where tobacco was readily available and they wanted to be assured of a means by which to smoke it. One colonist in the fort at this time was apparently so desperate for a pipe that he fashioned one out of brick!

More likely Cotton was sent by the Virginia Company to assay the clays for their potential in pipe and pottery making. This would fracture the monopoly held by the Dorset clay merchants for the London pipemaking industry and allow the investors to break into the lucrative pipe clay export to the Netherlands.

Perfumer

One perfumer, identified as Robert Alberton, was on the First Supply that reached Jamestown in January 1608. Perfume was relied upon heavily in 16th- and 17th-century Europe to help dispel the unsavory odors of unwashed bodies and refuse-laden streets. Scent was worn by both sexes, whether it was an herb or spice, such as the sweet marjoram favored by Queen Elizabeth, or waters distilled from aromatic plants. Perfumers produced a variety of scented preparations in liquid, dry, or salve form from the

Figure 46. A brick which has been modified for use as a tobacco pipe, probably using a reed for the stem.

43

Figure 47. A complete Border ware fuming pot from the Museum of London collections.

plants, or 'simples,' that grew wild or that were cultivated in herbal gardens. Like apothecaries, they must have had the skills and equipment for filtering, distilling, powdering, and blending various substances. The 1590 inventory of a perfumer in Ipswich, England, for instance, includes waters, oils, and ointments made of roses and chamomile, as well as the funnels, scales, and mortars needed to prepare them.[93]

The word *perfume* comes from the French *par fumer* or "by smoke," which hints at the original use of perfume as a burning substance, like incense, that would scent the air.[94] Aromatic substances would be dropped over smoldering coals, contained in a specialized vessel known as a fuming pot. One section of an earthenware fuming pot has been uncovered during the excavations. Also know as a stink pot or perfume jar, this form is a pedestalled cylindrical container with a narrow neck and pierced sides. The holes allow for the escape of the smoke or perfume of the substance, which has been placed on burning charcoal in the pot. A triangular opening in the pedestal base aids in the airflow to the burning coals. The fuming pot from James Fort is Red Border ware, produced in the potteries along the border of Hampshire and Surrey counties in England. While fuming pots are encountered in redware and silver, they are rare in Border ware.[95]

Figure 48. A section of a Red Border ware fuming pot from the James Fort excavations.

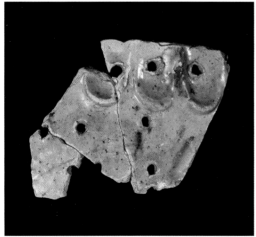

Stale air was thought to be unhealthy, and perfumers were employed to correct offensive environments. Shakespeare's character Borachio in *Much Ado About Nothing* refers to this role of perfumers when he says that he was "entertained [taken] for a perfumer, as I was smoking a musty room."[96] Because of the association of perfume with health, there was an overlap in the roles played by the apothecary and the perfumer. The royal apothecary, for example, was personally responsible for perfuming and fumigating all the monarch's clothes and bedding.[97]

Figure 49. The smoking chafing dish seen in the lower left corner of this painting is being used as a fuming pot to burn curative essences in the sick room.

Fumigating the sick with herbs had been practiced since ancient times in England and was especially popular during the medieval and early post-medieval periods. A proscribed "fume" in 1592 against the London plague consisted of "dried rosemary, juniper, bayleaves or frankincense burnt in a chafingdish and carried about from room to room."[98] Chafing dishes are footed bowls containing hot embers that were normally used to heat or warm a plate of food. In the absence of a fuming pot, a chafing dish would work quite nicely to contain smoldering essences.

The illness need not only be of the body to warrant fumigation. The *Grete Herball* published in 1526, which was a guide to the medicinal properties of simples, advises using the herb mugwort to treat an anxious child by making a "smoke therof under the chyldes's bedd." Further, if a patient should suffer from "weyknesse of the brayne," he should "receye the smoke" of rosemary "at his nose."[99]

By the time of Elizabeth, the practice of perfuming fabrics and dress accessories, particularly gloves and bags, had become popular. Leather gloves were worn by both men and women for almost every social occasion from dancing to fighting. Symbolic of trust and honor, gloves were often given as scented betrothal and wedding gifts.[100] This practice is reflected in Shakespeare's play *Much Ado about Nothing* when a courted female character states "those gloves the Count sent me, they are an excellent perfume."[101]

Figure 50. Gloves were popular dress accessories for both men and women in the 17th century and were often heavily scented with perfume.

A 17th-century recipe for perfuming gloves consists of gum-dragon, musk, civet, oil of cloves, cinnamon, and jasmine made into a paste to be rubbed into the leather.[102] It is interesting to note that the pair of "white lambe gloves" provided to each of the women who were sent to Virginia in 1621 to become wives for the settlers was purchased from

Figure 51. As depicted in this 17th-century Dutch painting, tailors customarily sat cross-legged upon a table while plying their craft.

a perfumer.[103] This indicates that the perfumers were in the business of selling accessories that they had treated with their special potions.

Why did the Virginia Company send Alberton to Jamestown? Even with the medicinal applications of "fumes," it is doubtful that Alberton was considered part of the medical team sent for the welfare of the colonists. It is much more likely that a perfumer was sent by the Virginia Company to search the woods for new simples that could be made into effective perfumes marketable in London.

Tailors

Figure 52. Until the late 17th century, tailors were usually men who made clothing for both men and women. Women, known as seamstresses, were confined to sewing the accessories.

Seven tailors are identified as arriving at Jamestown in the first year of settlement.[104] Three are never mentioned in the records again. Three are further named when they are drafted as soldiers by John Smith for expeditions in the summer and winter of 1608.[105] One of these individuals, William Ward, even had a landform named after him during one of the exploratory expeditions in which he participated.[106] One tailor, Thomas Hope, accompanies Smith and Newport to Powhatan's home at Werowocomoco in February 1608. On this listing he is identified as a gentleman and he is further identified as one of the authors of the Third Book of "The Proceedings."[107]

Tailors were trained in "the cutting up of a length of cloth and the shaping of it by cut and stitch to fit the contours of the human frame."[108] Their trade in England was primarily with individuals of the privileged classes and rarely with the average person who, except for perhaps one special garment, would wear homemade clothing. Textiles were expensive and clothing so valuable that it was often mentioned in wills and appraised in inventories.

Tailors could also apply their craft to the repair and modification of old garments, but it is unlikely that they were included on the voyage for the benefit of the average colonist. They are much more likely to have been in the employ of some of the gentlemen in the colony who were concerned that their social standing be correctly reflected in their wardrobes and in the servants they had to attend them. "A person of importance proclaimed his status by his choice of dress and jewels and by the number of liveried servants who accompanied him in public—the assumption being that the greater the number of retainers, the more important the man."[109]

Along with food, clothing was the most frequently requested commodity in the early years, starting in 1608 with Francis Perkins' pitiful plea for used clothing after a fire in the fort destroyed much of what the colonists had.[110] By the winter of 1613, the individuals at Jamestown state that it is no longer necessary to send food—now they need only clothing. In the same year, the Spanish spy Don Diego de Molina corroborates the "wretched clothing" that was worn by the individuals at Jamestown.[111]

Some of the tools traditionally used by tailors have been excavated from early contexts within James Fort and may relate to the presence of the first seven tailors. These include thimbles, needles, straight pins, pressing irons, and bodkins.

The word *thimble* is derived from the medieval English word *thymel* or *thuma* meaning thumb or thick finger.[112] This reflects its purpose as a protection for the finger in pushing a needle through fabric or leather. Twelve thimbles have been recovered from the excavations within James Fort. They represent the two types depicted by the 17th-century chronicler of material culture, Randle Holme[113]—the ring or open-ended thimble and those with closed ends.

Nine of the James Fort thimbles are made

Figure 53. Two types of thimbles are depicted in Randle Holme's Academy of Armory & Blazon. Although this book was not published until 1688, Holme finished the work for it in 1649.

Figure 54. Brass Nuremberg thimble found in the bulwark trench of James Fort. There is a maker's mark in the symbol of a bell just above the decorative band of foliage.

Figure 55. Brass ring thimble from Pit 3, ca. 1610, which has an undecipherable maker's mark.

Figure 56. Group of brass doublet buttons and an iron ring thimble that were found joined together in Pit 1.

of brass and six of them were recovered from the same pre-1610 context in the cellar fill of Structure 165. These all appear to be of Nuremberg manufacture. By the middle of the 16th century, the city of Nuremberg in Germany prevailed in the production of small brass objects, particularly thimbles. This dominance is primarily attributable to the discovery of a high quality brass, produced by alloying copper and zinc, "which created a smooth bright brass of an even texture."[114] Also, the Nuremberg craftsmen developed a technique by the end of the 16th century of making two-part thimbles. This simplified the process of decorating the thimbles as it could be done while they were in flat sheets. The sides were then rolled into cylinders and soldered together and the cap was similarly attached on the top edge. The prior technique had involved heating the brass and punching it into molds. Any decoration then had to be applied by hand to the molded thimble.

Nuremberg thimbles typically are tall and narrow with a flat or only slightly rounded top. They are punched by hand around the sides in a spiral that continues over the top. Often, these thimbles bear decorative stamping around the border and/or maker's marks in the way of initials or symbols. So far, these marks are not linked to individual makers.

Three of the ring thimbles are iron and one is of brass. This type of thimble is usually associated with working heavy, thick fabrics such as sailcloth, although one of the excavated iron ring thimbles was concreted to nine copper alloy doublet buttons. A doublet is a closely fitting man's jacket, which is fastened down the front, from neck to waist, by many closely spaced buttons. The buttons found with the thimble still contained remnants of the thread which had once strung them together, suggesting that these objects had been stored together, possibly in a pouch, as a small repair kit. Perhaps the kit had also once contained a needle which, being thin and iron, may have rusted away.

Figure 57. Three of the over 300 17th-century brass straight pins from James Fort.

Eleven iron needles, ranging in size from 40 mm to 59 mm have been excavated from the site thus far. They all exhibit a round-sectioned shank tapering to a point, but the eye on each of the examples is either broken out or lost. These needles would have been used for regular sewing. Larger needles would be used for repairing fishing nets.

Because of the metal's durability in the ground, brass straight pins are much more common on archaeological sites than needles. Over 300 pins and another 100 pin fragments, without heads, have been recovered from James Fort. These range in length from 30 mm to 51 mm. Pins were used extensively in the

17th century, not only in the process of constructing garments, but also to hold some clothing, particularly accessories, together. They are also commonly found in Virginia's colonial-period burials where they were used to fasten the cloth shroud wrapping the body.

The technology for pin manufacture remained much the same from the mid-16th century to the 19th century. Drawn brass wire was used for the shaft, which was cut into short lengths and filed to a sharp point. A length of wire wound on the shaft in two complete turns made the globular head. In the late 18th century, heading wire was thinner than the

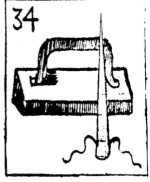

Figure 58. A tailor's pressing iron and a needle depicted by Randle Holme.

shank and was usually wound five times to form a conical head. In the beginning of the 19th century, the modern form of pin was introduced whereby a solid head is fabricated using part of the shank.[115]

England imported most of its straight pins from the Netherlands in the medieval and early post-medieval periods.[116] Pins could be produced more cheaply there for two basic reasons: proximity to brass production areas along the river Meuse and lower labor costs, because the industry was not controlled by guilds as it was in England.[117]

Two types of irons have been found in the excavations. One consists of a flat heavy piece of iron with a handle that Randle Holme depicts as a "Taylors pressing iron." This type would be heated over the fire before use and presumably picked up using a cloth or some other protection wrapped around the handle. Another ironing device, known as a goffering iron, was used in England in the 17th and 18th centuries. To goffer means to crimp or frill, and these tools were necessary to maintain the large cartwheel neck ruff that was popular men's fashion from ca.1580-1610. The goffered bands of linen were sometimes so large that they had to be sup-

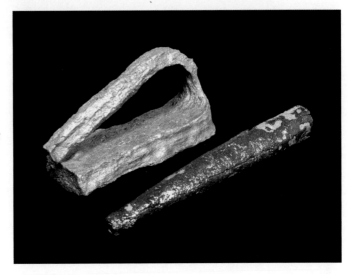

Figure 59. A goffering iron and pressing iron from the excavations.

49

Figure 60. Seventeenth-century portrait depicting the fashionable large ruffs which required frequent treatment with a goffering iron to maintain their shape.

ported by an inner wire frame, known as a supportasse. The goffering iron, or *poking stick*, consisted of a tube that was heated by inserting a red-hot iron of a slightly smaller diameter. The material to be ironed would first have to be stiffened with white starch and then pressed over the heated tube to make a semicircular fold.

The presence of a goffering iron within the confines of James Fort is yet another suggestion that the gentlemen continued to dress the same way they had at home. As mentioned earlier, it was very important in English society at the time to maintain distinctions of class, rank, and profession by the clothes that one wore and the objects one possessed. Obviously, these customs of conspicuous display were maintained in the

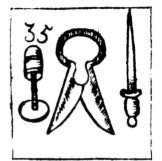

isolated, military colony, far removed from the society that they would most impress.

The starch,[118] that was so important to maintaining the fashionable ruffs, is known from the historic records to have been used at Jamestown, although not always in the way that it was originally intended. George Percy, the "highest born gentleman of the settlement" requests that his brother in London send him £4/6/0 worth of "Starche" in July 1608.[119] This is presumably for the treatment of the "apparrell of diuerse sewts" worth over £32 that was also a part of Percy's order. Perhaps this same starch helped Percy to survive the Starving Time winter of 1609-1610, for John Smith tells us food supplies were so low that "those that had starch for their ruffs made a gluey porridge of it."[120]

Holme depicts another tailoring tool known as a bodkin. He describes this object as "a blade or round Pin of Iron fixed in a Halve, it is not very sharp at the end: by its help, is Eye lid (eyelet) holes and all other holes, (which are not very large) made."[121]

The tailor's bodkin is an awl-like tool used to make the holes in clothing, through which the laces used to bind or secure a garment are threaded. One handle of a tailor's bodkin has been found within James Fort. It consists of half of a cast brass handle that would secure the tang of the bodkin. The handle is deeply molded with three figures: starting from the top is a demi-figure of a woman with her arms folded on hr lap, a lion's head holding a ring through its mouth, and a crowned female figure in Elizabethan clothes.[122]

The "eye lid" or eyelet holes mentioned by Holme are also known as aglet holes. Aglets (also known as tags or points) are the metal tips folded on the ends of the laces. A modern corollary for this object is the plastic tip that is fitted on the ends of shoelaces and that serves to keep the lace ends from fraying. Laces were used to secure many parts of 17th-century clothing. The hose that men wore, for instance, were held up by an average of nine pair of laces, requiring two aglets each, which were threaded through holes at the waist of the doublet.[123]

Aglets were, for the most part, functional and were constructed of unadorned copper alloy, as are most of the nearly 1,000 aglets excavated from James Fort. But they were also used for decorative effect and dangled from all parts of gentlemen's clothing. Some of the aglets excavated from James Fort are of the decorative type and are stamped with a waffle or dot and diaper motif. One is even constructed of silver and is decorated with stars in a scale pattern.

Figure 61. A bodkin (right) is illustrated by Randle Holme with shears and another tailor's tool, known as a scorer, whereby the fabric is marked before cutting.

Figure 62. Ornately cast bodkin handle from Pit 1.

Figure 63. Plain copper alloy aglets.

51

Figure 64. Aglets can be seen at this gentleman's waist. They are securing his trousers through holes in his jacket.

Another class of artifact that has been found during the James Fort excavations also relates to tailors in its association with fabric. Small leaden devices known as cloth seals were part of the European textile industry's system of industrial regulation and quality control between the 14th and 19th centuries. Manufacturers and finishers of cloth, as well as merchants and tax officials, once crimped these diminutive objects onto textiles as they moved through the various processes from loom to consumer.[124]

The most common type of cloth seal is two-part, consisting of a disc with a tapered rivet (disc 1) connected by a thin strip to a similarly sized disc with a central hole (disc 2). The seal is folded at the connecting strip over the edge of fabric "so that the rivet on one disc could be pushed through the fabric and the corresponding hole in the other disc."[125] The discs were sealed firmly over the cloth through being stamped with one, or between two, dies which impressed the discs with various numerals, letters, and/or decorative motifs.

Figure 65. Elizabethan alnage seal depicting the Tudor arms.

Fifty-four cloth seals have been excavated from James Fort. The various impressions upon the seals can provide a good deal of information beyond that of simply identifying the types of material the colonists were using. Status can be indicated, as well as suggestions of trading patterns and practices. One of the seals (1216-JR), for instance, is an Elizabethan alnage seal impressed with the Tudor coat of arms. The alnager is the crown's official representative who insures that the proper taxes have been paid on the textile. This particular impression would not have been used beyond 1602, the year of Elizabeth's death, being at that time replaced by the symbols of James I. Since the Jamestown colony did not start until 1607 this means that the textile must have been produced at least 5 years before it reached Virginia. This is a surprisingly long time for the fabric to be languishing about unused, considering the high value of textiles in the 17th century. A lot of capital was tied up in the production and distribution of cloth, and all indications are that textiles were sold and subsequently used soon after production.[126]

Another Elizabethan seal (1112-JR) appears to be from the county of Kent, which was a major producer of kersey and broadcloth during the late 16th and early 17th centuries. Broadcloth is a fine traditional woolen textile used primarily for men's clothing in England from the 12th century. The previously mentioned Jamestown gentleman George Percy ordered "6 yardes of Broade Clothe for a Cloke a Jerkin and a paire of breeches."[127]

Eight alnage seals dating to the period of Elizabeth's reign have been excavated during the *Jamestown Rediscovery* project. One seal (520-JR) even bears a date of the 1590s, although the last digit is obscured. The frequency of these early seals (15%) indicates a pattern of textile supply to the colony consisting of old stores of material. These supplies had perhaps been assembled for previous voyages of the merchant adventurers that abounded during Elizabeth's reign and continued under James. Possibly the goods were not used during the journey and were off-loaded at London on the return voyage to be stored for another venture. A court

Figure 66. One of two privy seals that have been found in James Fort with the initials RB.

minute from the East India Company dated September 1607 appears to substantiate this practice. It records "beads *and cloth very much moth eaten*, sold to the Governor Sir Thomas Smythe for L3.5s. for the Virginia Voyage."[128] The beads were clearly intended for the Indian trade, but was the cloth as well? Perhaps the English considered the Indians to be undiscriminating consumers who would accept fabric no matter what the condition. Or was Smythe trying to save his undercapitalized Virginia Company some money by clothing the colonists in hole-ridden textiles? Smythe, a highly successful London merchant, had controlling interests in both the East India Company, of which he was governor, and the Virginia Company, of which he was the treasurer and the first chief executive. He would be aiding both organizations by buying up the unused supplies from one group that would be needed by the other. It is likely that the East India Company surplus is also the source of the inadequate tents about which John Smith complains.[129] The Virginia Company pattern of supplying its colony with second rate goods seems to endure its tenure. As late as 1623, colonists are grumbling that they are being "victualed wth mustie bred the reliques of former Vioages."[130]

Other cloth seals found are known as privy seals. They were used by weavers, merchants, and dyers and usually include initials in conjunction with the stylized privy or *huismerk*. This mark consists of the number 4, sometimes depicted backwards, on the top of a vertical line that terminates in two side-by-side "x's." Initials are usually ligatured or astride the mark.

The privy mark was *a sort of commercial heraldry* used quite commonly from the early 16th century.[131] They are believed to have begun as marks of property in northern and central Europe when most of the individuals were illiterate. They were then adapted by Dutch and English merchants as trademarks—an easily recognizable guarantee of quality.[132] Very few of these marks have been identified with English merchants, so the dating of these seals must be primarily by the style of the mark and letters.[133]

Figure 67. Dyers' seal from London stamped with SEARCHED indicating that the cloth had been officially inspected.

One dyers' guild seal (656-JR) contains the word *SEARCHED*, which indicates that the cloth had been inspected. Less visible are the large letters W—A D which probably stands for WOADED, which is a blue colored dye.[134] An inspector of the guild certifying that the dye was up to standard would have applied this seal.

A number of the cloth seals from James Fort are associated with German fabrics that had

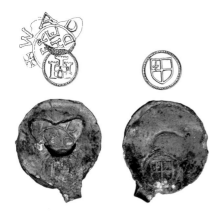

been imported into England, probably through London, before being shipped to Virginia. Imported textiles are generally types that were not produced in England, but occasionally they are fabrics that could be obtained more cheaply abroad. From the lead seals that have been recorded in England, only one in forty is foreign, which indicates that Continental imports were not very prevalent.[135]

Figure 68. Cloth seal exhibiting the pinecone and letter A, representing Augsburg, Germany.

Five of the seals bear the letter *A* and the pinecone heraldic badge of the southern German city of Augsburg. This type, known in over a dozen English counties, is the most common of the Continental cloth seals recovered in England, comprising one third of the identified assemblage.[136] Augsburg seals have also been recovered at Martin's Hundred, the neighboring settlement to Jamestown. There, eight seals were excavated from ca.1620–1622 contexts and represent the most closely dated Augsburg seals prior to the Jamestown finds.[137] In Britain they are generally dated between the late 16th and middle 17th century, by which time "the import of German fabrics was seriously curtailed."[138]

Augsburg was known for its production of fustian, which is a mixed linen-warp/cotton-weft fabric. Fustian could be made with a silky finish and was often used as a substitute for velvet.[139] In 1610, Virginia colonist George Percy ordered from England "3 yardes 1 quarter of fustian for a dublett and Joanes fustian to lyn…4 suites & a dublett and a paire of clothe breeches."[140] Percy was a gentleman, who, at the time of this request, had been newly elected President of the colony. His doublets and breeches would necessarily be made of a fabric reflective of his rank in society. There is a reference in William Shakespeare's *Taming of the Shrew*, which is believed to have been written sometime between 1594 and 1606, to the "serving men in their new fustian."[141] In this case, the servants are clothed in this textile as an indication of the household's status.

Another Continental cloth seal from the site comes from the Baltic city of Gdansk, which was part of Germany in the 17th century, but is now within Poland. Disc 1 of the two-part seal consists of the number "56" over an "E" on a garnished shield. This most likely represents the length of the cloth in ells.[142] Disc 2 bears the arms of Gdansk, consisting of a crown over two crosses potent on a shield. This cloth seal was probably attached to sailcloth. "In the late 16th century and the early 17th century, some 5 percent by value of England's imports from the Baltic were canvasses for sailmaking, mainly brought from Gdansk to London."[143] The Jamestown colonists would have need of sailcloth to repair the sails on their shallops and other boats rigged for

Figure 69. Cloth seal from Gdansk.

sailing. They also evidently had need of sailcloth for shelter, as illustrated by John Smith's description of the first church at Jamestown. *When I went first to Virginia, I well remember, wee did hang an awning (which is an old saile) to three or foure trees to shadow us from the Sunne . . . this was our Church.*[144]

Cooper

Figure 70. The cooper was essential to the colony for producing the containers by which goods could be shipped back to England.

One cooper identified as John Lewes was included in the first supply of 1608. Cooperage was important to the colony for producing the containers needed to store and transport goods. Wooden barrels or casks would have provided the most satisfactory storage for the colony's provisions, although they could not prevent spoilage in the extremes of the Virginia climate. Without the modern convenience of refrigeration, storing up a surplus of foodstuffs for later consumption was nearly impossible for the colonists. As John Smith disappointingly relates in one instance, "In searching our casked corn wee found it halfe rotten."[145]

Figure 71. Randle Holme's depiction of a croze with the iron in place.

Lewes would have been busy from the very beginning trying to keep up with the need for barrels to contain the immediately available commodities such as "Sasafrix roots,"[146] which members of the council described as being their "easiest and richest comodity."[147] It was so easy that the sailors returning to England in June 1607 had gathered up two tons of it as contraband. Not only did they break some of the colony's tools in the process of digging the sassafras roots, but they also upset Jamestown's trade of the commodity by flooding the London market!

Containers were also needed for the substances that the colonists would eventually produce to ship back to England. In a three month period, for example, John Smith records the production of "3 or 4 last of pitch and tar." A *last* is a commercial capacity, and for pitch it refers to between 12 and 14 barrels.[148]

Figure 72. A cooper's croze iron found in Pit 1.

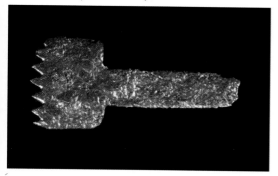

The critical wood shortage in England, resulting from shipbuilding and the massive use of wood as industrial fuel for the production of iron, made Virginia's forests look very attractive to the colony's investors. The colonists noted that the Jamestown area was:
generally replenish'd with wood of all kinds and that the fairest, yea, and best that ever any of us (traveler or workman) ever saw,

56

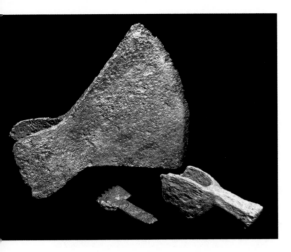

Figure 73. A broad axe and an adze along with the croze iron (center), which would have been required by the cooper in the process of his work.

being fit for any use whatsoever, as ships, house, planks, pales, boards, masts, wainscot, clapboard – for pikes or elsewhat.[149]

Among the first commodities sent back to England, and one that would continue to be exported for some time, was "a taste of Clapboard."[150] Clapboard refers to the short, split oak staves used to make barrels. In the production of a barrel, the clapboard or staves are curved by heating and are bound together by hoops of wood or iron, which are forced down over them. The top and bottom of the barrel sits securely in a groove known as a croze, which is produced near the interior ends of the staves. The tool used to produce the groove is also called a croze, the iron element of which has been recovered from the fort.

Besides the croze, a kit of cooper's tools would also include a broad axe, for dressing the cut wood, and a small adze, to cut the beveled ends of the barrel. Both of these tools have been found in the excavations and, along with the croze iron, may have belonged to Virginia's first cooper, John Lewes.

Figure 74. Wood was one of Virginia's greatest assets, and carpenters were needed by the colony to prepare it for export, as well as to build Jamestown's structures.

Carpenters

Although all the men, even the gentlemen, were engaged in felling trees and the making of wainscot and clapboard, there were four carpenters on the first ship. It is interesting that Smith made soldiers of all four and thereby kept them from exercising their craft. One, William Laxon, was even given the title "Ensign," presumably taking over the duty of flag bearer from Ensign Jerome Alikock, who "died of a wound" on August 14, 1607. Two others, Robert Small and Edward Pising, had points of land named after them to commemorate their participation with Smith on journeys of exploration. Small only went on one of these forays, but Pising accompanied Smith on two—in July and December of 1608—and thereby earned himself the title of sergeant by the second expedition. The fourth carpenter was not so lucky. Thomas Emery was slain by Indians while on a December 1607 excursion with Smith.

Figure 75. Collection of carpenters' tools recovered from James Fort, including dividers, a felling axe, a hatchet, a socket chisel, and two files.

From all this military activity, it appears that the carpenters were not spending much time building structures. Personal dwellings were not a priority in James Fort anyway. By September 1607, a full four months after arrival, the president of the colony was still in a tent.[151] Even in January 1608, the First Supply arrived to find the colonists "utterly destitute of houses, not one as yet built, so that they lodged in cabins and holes within the ground."[152]

The colonists appear to have followed one of the directives of the Virginia Company, which stated that "before any house be set up for any private person" all "carpenters and suchlike workmen" should be put to work erecting public buildings, such as the storehouse. The next bit of instruction is very interesting for the information it reveals about the relationship between the men in the colony. It states, "and though the workmen *may belong to any private persons, yet let them all work together first for the company and then for private men.*"[153] The craftsmen, then, were not necessarily Company men but were in the employ of some of the gentlemen in the group. They were part of the voyage to serve and provide comfort, and perhaps profit, for their masters and not to sustain or produce income for the Virginia Company.

Laxon, Pising, Small, and Emery may have been in the employ of one or more of the gentlemen that accompanied Smith on his expeditions, which would also explain their inclusion in the trips. It appears, at any rate, that three of them may have been no more than apprentices, for the historical records say that up until the Third Supply there was, "but one Carpenter in the Countrey and three others that could doe little, but desired to be learners."[154]

Woodworking tools such as felling axes, dividers, hatchets, chisels, wedges, and files have been found in the excavations.

Figure 76. The blacksmith would have been needed for all manner of ironworking at Jamestown, from the repair of weaponry and tools to the shoeing of horses. A pile of iron to be recycled , including what appears to be a piece of arm armor called a vambrace, can be seen on this 17ᵗʰ-century blacksmith's floor.

Blacksmiths

One blacksmith is listed as arriving with the first group of settlers in 1607, although a second blacksmith and a gunsmith follow on the First Supply in January 1608. As workers of iron, both blacksmiths and the gunsmith would have had similar training and most likely worked together at Jamestown to repair firearms and other weaponry, as well as tools. Only the first blacksmith, James Read, receives further mention after his arrival, and a colorful reference it is. In September 1607, he is almost hanged. According to Edward Maria Wingfield, the newly deposed president of the council, the punishment is for returning a blow from President John Ratcliffe.[155] John Smith says Read was sentenced for cursing at Ratcliffe and threatening "to strike him with some of his tooles."[156] In any case, Read literally saved his own neck by divulging that fellow colonist Captain George Kendall was planning a mutiny. Kendall is executed for his alleged conspiracies, but Read goes on to accompany John Smith on a couple of exploratory expeditions in June and December 1608. On one of those journeys with Smith to chart the landscape, he even had a point of land named after him.[157]

One has to wonder why a craftsman with an occupation so useful to the daily life of the colony is off on risky trips with Smith. Is it possible that he also came to Jamestown under the sponsorship of one of the gentlemen in the fort—one who had possibly died in the first few months, thereby leaving his servant as a free agent? One likely gentleman is Dru Pickhouse (Piggase) who died in August 1607. Before coming to Virginia, Pickhouse owned and managed an iron forge on his family's Sussex County estate.[158] It is tempting, with both Pickhouse and Read arriving at the same time and with both men involved in iron working, to associate the two. With Pickhouse's early demise, Read would have been subject to the whims of the council members who were leading the colony and would be, thereby, available for soldiering.

Pickhouse appears to have had financial woes in England, which may explain why he left a wife and two children to go to Jamestown. He had been in debtor's prison in the 1590s for failing to pay for wood to fuel his forge, and by 1601 he was forced to sell the family manor.[159] Perhaps he participated in the first venture with the hopes that he could use the abundant forests to reestablish a profitable iron forge—one, hopefully, in which he would not have to pay for the wood!

The production of iron in the colony was a driving interest of the Virginia Company investors. In December 1608, Smith, then president, sends them "two barrels of stones" which he believes "to be good Iron ore." The "stones" are coming from more than one source, as Smith says that he has included notes describing where he found each sample.[160] Smith appears to have had faith in Virginia's potential for iron production. In his opinion, the colony's "best commoditie was Yron," which he says they "made into little chissels."[161] This iron was probably the naturally occurring bog iron or limonite, a hydrated form of iron oxide, which is plentiful along the James River banks. The bog ore would have been treated in a small furnace known as a bloomery, which required little labor but could produce only modest amounts of iron.[162] In a bloomery, "the ore was heated to form a semi-molten mass or bloom of wrought iron, which was refined by hammering on the anvil."[163]

The anvil is one of the most important components of a blacksmith's equipment. Comprising a heavy piece of metal that has maintained the same basic shape through the centuries, it is the surface upon which the iron is worked. A pointed element that projects from one or both sides of the anvil, known as a horn, has been excavated from a plowzone layer in James Fort. The horn is "used to curve pieces of iron for shaping rings, links, shackles and other round or curving objects."[164] Since the anvil horn comes from the plowzone, which is a mixed context, it is not known if it is associated with the earliest blacksmiths in the colony.

An element of an anvil, known as a hardy, was excavated in 1955 by National Park Service archaeologists from an area within the Confederate earthwork that lies under and beside James Fort.[165] A hardy is a wedge-shaped tool with a square sectioned tang that fits in a hole in the anvil. The cutting edge of the hardy makes an "impact on the underside of the work when the smith strikes it from above."[166] The hardy was found in association with forge refuse including slag, smithing scrap, and evidence of

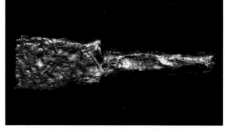

Figure 77. An anvil hardy that was excavated from the vicinity of James Fort by National Park Service archaeologists in 1955.

weapon repair, that is believed to date to the first quarter of the 17th century.[167] It is not known how this feature relates to those of James Fort that have been excavated by the APVA, but this will be determined by excavations planned for the future.

The smiths in James Fort would be called upon for the repair of both military and non-military iron objects, the manufacture of tools, nails, and other small objects, as well as for the shoeing of the horses. By the summer of 1609 there were six mares and two horses,[168] but there have been no horseshoes found in the excavations to indicate that they had been shod. It would have been a needless exercise anyway as the colonists ate all the horses at Jamestown over the Starving Time winter of 1609-1610.

There is evidence of another activity that most logically would have been assigned to the smiths—recycling of the plate armor. For the body armor known as a cuirass, consisting of a backplate and breastplate, to be effective protection it had to be worn by the soldier whenever there was a threat of danger. In the early years of the

Figure 78. A breastplate that has been cut up into jackplates, and a soldier wearing a coat of jacks (left).

colony, this was all the time, which made it very uncomfortable for the colonists to perform such routine tasks as hunting or cutting wood. In addition, the heavy body protection was a detriment to quick maneuvers when involved in skirmishes with the Native Americans. John Smith revealed this handicap when he noted that "the Salvages are so light and swift, though we see them (being so loaded with armour) they have much advantage of us though they be cowards."[169]

Only one intact breastplate has been recovered from the site. Another has been reshaped into a container, perhaps a cooking pot or pail, reflecting new priorities for the colonists. Conversion of plate armor is also evident in the numerous pieces that have been cut to produce another type of body protection, known as a coat of jacks. A coat of jacks would have resembled the tight-fitting man's jacket called a doublet, but the material would have been strong and coarse like canvas or buckram. Sewn or quilted between the two layers of the coat are over 1,000 small square or oblong metal plates, known as jacks. The Spanish also had these garments which they called *escaupile* and which they found to be very effective against Indian arrows. Spaniard Gonzalo Mendez de Canzo tells the Spanish king in 1600 that "as for war with Indians no other armour except (the escaupile) is of any value." He goes on to explain that arrows can pierce coats of mail, as they can leather buff coats. They can rebound dangerously from plate armor, perhaps injuring a colleague; but *it is clear that the escupil is the best armour because the arrow is stopped by it and sticks.*[170]

Glassmakers

Glassmakers arrived at Jamestown on September 29, 1608, aboard the *Mary and Margaret.* Two months later, this ship returned to London freighted with Virginia commodities, among them a "tryal of glasse." The glassmakers had been under pressure to produce proof to their English sponsors that the ingredients necessary to produce glass were available in the Jamestown area. Evidence of this two-month effort is abundant within the fort's early features in the way of crucibles—some containing molten glass or sand—large melting pots with glass residues, and pounds of cullet, or waste glass. John Smith acknowledges the industriousness of these glassworkers when he mentions that most of the "labourers" in the fort "never did know what a dayes worke was, except the Dutch-men [Deutschmänner or German] and Poles, and some dozen other."[171]

The glassmakers have long been thought to be from Poland or individuals from both Poland and Germany.[172] Just as in the previous quote, the two ethnic groups are frequently mentioned in the same breath in the Jamestown records. This is possibly because both crews of men spoke little or no English, and this set them apart from the rest of the colonists. The linkage of the Poles and Germans starts with John Smith's list of the Second Supply, which records the arrival of "eight Dutch men and

Figure 79. Evidence of the glassmakers at work within the fort prior to 1610.

Poles."[173] Another statement by John Smith criticizes the Virginia Company's search "into Germany or Poleland for glasse-men and the rest."[174] What Smith means by "the rest" is revealed in another quote when he mentions "the hyring of the Poles and Dutchmen to make Pitch, Tar…and Sope ashes," as well as glass.[175]

Scholars now believe that the Germans were the glassmakers and the Poles were the producers of "the rest"—the pitch, tar, and soap ashes.[176] Of the eight Germans and Poles mentioned, we know that three were German and we know their first names—Adam, Samuel, and Francis. There were traditionally only two or three men in a glassmaking team,[177] so the remaining five men were probably all Polish. At times the Germans and Poles would have had to work in tandem, which may be another reason that the two groups are often linked. The Poles' soap ash, which is also known as potash,[178] is potassium carbonate. Made from the ashes of wood, potash provides the alkali that is required to help melt glass ingredients together and create a stable product. Since the glassmakers at Jamestown were using wood for fuel, they would eventually have a constant supply of the potash they needed in the ashes their furnaces produced. In the beginning, however, they would have need of some of the potash produced by the Polish laborers before they could start work. English glassmakers during this time period faced a worse problem. They had to purchase potash from European sources, as they were being forced by legislation to convert to coal, which produced no wood ash, as their source of fuel.

As mentioned, a so-called trial of glass was returned to England at the end of 1608. It is not known for sure what comprised that test, but it was probably no more than a glass ingot providing proof of the efficacy of Virginia's glassmaking resources. The glassmakers intended product is believed to have been window glass. There was an enormous window shortage in London, as "large expanses of glass were becoming fashionable for those who could afford them."[179] Window glass had to be imported from the continent at great cost to meet the demand because English glassmakers in the beginning of the 17th century could not make window glass profitably using coal furnaces. The Virginia Company felt that a window glass factory in Virginia would be a lucrative enterprise, despite the breakage that would occur during transport. There was a limitless supply of wood for fueling the furnaces and producing potash, as well as plenty of sand on the James River beaches to provide the needed silica.

Besides sand and potash, another ingredient was used in the production of glass—cullet or waste glass. Old broken glass or scraps of glass formed during the manufacturing process were thrown into the mix to reduce the melting point. This was economical for the glassmakers because they would not have to sustain high temperatures in their furnaces, the same reason that glass is recycled today. Over 7,000 fragments of cullet have been recovered along with other glassmaking debris in the fort. The fragments are all pieces of crown window glass, probably brought from a European window factory. Crown glass is blown glass that has been spun on the end of a long rod, called a pontil, into large flat disks that could be 2 - 3' in diameter. There was a lot of waste with this type of glass when the glazier cut the rounds into panes to lead into a window. The curved, raised edge pieces and the thickened center where the pontil had been attached, known as the bull's eye, were unusable. These waste elements from the round would be collected from the workshop floor to be sold as the commodity known as cullet.

Figure 80. An 18th-century illustration showing how crown glass was spun into large rounds.

Figure 80. Crown glass round scored into panes of glass. The center "bull's eye" and the edge pieces are unsuitable for placing in a window and are discarded as cullet.

The German glassmakers were producing green glass or *Waldglas*, which was the typical type of glass produced using potash in the forest glasshouses of the 16th and 17th centuries. The green color is a result of the high amount of iron oxide in the impure beach sand that was the source of silica. Decolorizing agents that could neutralize the green color were known, however they have not been associated thus far with the making of forest glass.[180] Several pieces of one of these minerals, pyrolusite or manganese oxide, were found in association with the glassmaking artifacts in James Fort.[181] The properties of pyrolusite were known as early as the mid-16th century when metalworker Vannoccio Biringuccio described that the substance "cleanses melted glass when it is mixed with it and causes it to change from green or yellow to white."[182] The achievement of a lighter glass would be highly desirable in the production of glass for windows, as this material would permit more light to penetrate the dimly lit 17th-century interiors. Biringuccio goes on to say that this material comes from Germany and Northern Italy.[183]

Also from Germany are the refractory clay crucibles that were used to melt the raw materials. The clay of these crucibles has quartz sand as a main ingredient and is fired to a near-stoneware consistency that creates "industrial strength" vessels able to withstand very high heat without breakage. One of the crucibles is marked twice on the base with a circular stamp bearing the initials PTV GER. Crucibles with this same mark have been recorded from excavations in Grossalmerode near Kassel, Germany. Indeed, the GER stands for Gross—almerode, a primary center of glass and crucible production for 400 years that peaked in the early 17th century. The PTV is believed to represent Peter Topfer, who was listed as a leaseholder in the

Figure 81. Close-up of pyrolusite brought by glassmakers to decolorize glass.

crucible production monopoly from 1621-1625. He is named "the elder" in 1621, so he was most likely making crucibles prior to the 1608 glassmaking activity at Jamestown.[184]

With all the byproducts of glassmaking in the fort and additional subsequent efforts apparent in the glasshouse on Glasshouse Point,[185] there is yet no evidence that the German glassmakers ever succeeded in making anything. The main obstacle appears to have been the insufficiency of food in the colony and the growing lack of confidence the German craftsmen had that their English employers could sustain them. Immediately after the departure of the ship carrying the glass sample to London in December 1608, John Smith sent the Germans to build a house for Powhatan because he had "no victuals to imploy them" in the fort. Without food in their stomachs, Smith says, "few were able to doe any thing to purpose."[186] While living with the Indians, the Germans were not only well fed, but they were led to believe that Powhatan was planning an attack on the fort to take advantage of the weakened condition of the colonists. Thinking that the settlement could not survive a double hit of hunger and an Indian assault, they decided that they would have a better chance of survival with Powhatan and agreed to smuggle arms and tools out of the fort for him. These intrigues consumed the better part of 1609, with the end result that all three Germans were dead at the hands of the Indians by the next spring. There was no time and little incentive to make glass.

Figure 82. Crucible base from bulwark trench stamped twice with a maker's mark PTV/GER, representing Peter Topfer, Grossalmerode, Germany.

 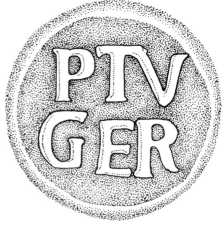

Conclusions

Just as in the children's choosing rhyme,

> *Tinker, tailor, soldier, sailor,*
> *rich man, poor man, beggar man, thief,*
> *doctor, lawyer, Indian chief"*

a wide range of occupations and social positions is reflected in the individuals at Jamestown during the first one and a half years of settlement. The "Indian chief" is, of course, Powhatan who never set foot on Jamestown Island once the colonists arrived, but who, as leader of the vast empire of Indian groups that surrounded the English colony, played a major role in the Jamestown story. But what is known about the rest of the individuals?

Most of the Jamestown experience is reflected through the eyes of the "rich men" and the individuals who had professions requiring university training, such as the "doctors" and the "lawyers." These, for the most part, were the literates—the ones who either wrote the accounts or who were considered by their peers to be interesting enough to write about. An obvious exception to this is John Smith, a professional soldier, who left us the largest body of literature regarding the early years at Jamestown. "As a writer, John Smith apologized for *his owne rough pen*, yet he left to posterity…an invaluable, if one-sided contemporary history of early Virginia."[187]

The men who couldn't write their own accounts have nonetheless left stories for us to interpret by way of the trash they generated while going about their everyday lives. In it we find remnants of their weaponry and tools, remains of their meals, fragments of their pottery and glassware, pieces of their jewelry and clothing, and bits of their musical instruments and games. Put all together, this material record presents a picture of life that is so much more than the static generalization of laziness and incompetence that has found its way onto the pages of the history books. This is about living, breathing individuals who risked their lives for various reasons to travel to a new frontier. Some of the reasons were for adventure, some for opportunity, some to escape overwhelming personal problems, and some because they probably had little choice. We know from the records that some came as servants—John Smith had his page Samuel Collier whom he sent to live among the Indians to learn their language, and Captain John Martin had his scribe Anas Todkill whom he had commanded to "record his journies."[188] A good number of the craftsmen and laborers were also probably in the colony under the sponsorship of some of the gentlemen who were accustomed to having their retinue of serving men around them. These servants came prepared to work, as indicated by the archaeological remains.

So why did the colony almost fail? Why was Jamestown almost abandoned just three years after it was first settled? John Smith tells us that it was the Virginia Company's drive to achieve immediate returns for the investors that worked to the detriment of the colony's welfare. He stated that "for in overtoiling our weak and unskillful bodies in this desire for present profit we can scarce ever recover ourselves from one supply to the next."

The Virginia Company, which eventually lost its charter in 1624, would have done well to heed the words of Sir Francis Bacon:

> Planting of countries is like planting of Woods; for you must make account to lose almost twenty years' profit, and expect your recompense in the end: for the principal thing that hath been the destruction of most plantations, has been the base and hasty drawing of profit in the first years.[189]

Appendix

Name	Occupation	Arrival	References
James Read	Blacksmith	May 13, 1607	September 1607: strikes President Ratcliffe and is almost hanged; implicates Kendall in conspiracies against colony; June 2, 1608: soldier; December 29, 1608: soldier; Read's Point named after him
Richard Dole	Blacksmith	January 2, 1608	
John Herd	Bricklayer	May 13, 1607	
Edward Short	Bricklayer	May 13, 1607	May 1607 listed as Ould Edward, laborer; Wingfield says that he visited "old Short the bricklayer"
William Garrett	Bricklayer	May 13, 1607	
William Laxon	Carpenter	May 13, 1607	Spring 1609: Ensign, sent down river to live upon oysters
Edward Pising	Carpenter	May 13, 1607	July 20, 1608: soldier; December 29, 1608: sergeant; Pising's Point named after him
Thomas Emery	Carpenter	May 13, 1607	December 10, 1607: slain by Indians while on an excursion with Smith
Robert Small	Carpenter	May 13, 1607	July 20, 1608: soldier; Small's Point named after him
John Lewes	Cooper	January 2, 1608	
Richard Keale	Fishmonger	Not known	June 2, 1608: soldier and fishmonger; Keale's Hill ("the highest land on the main, yet it was but low") named after him; July 20, 1608: soldier
Adam	Glassmaker	September 29, 1608	December 1608: sent to build Powhatan a home; May 1610 killed by Indians
Francis	Glassmaker	September 29, 1608	December 1608: sent to build Powhatan a home; Winter 1609 killed by Indians
Samuel	Glassmaker	September 29, 1608	December 1608: sent to build Powhatan a home; May 1610 killed by Indians
William Johnson	Goldsmith	January 2, 1608	
Richard Belfield	Goldsmith	January 2, 1608	
Peter Keffer	Gunsmith	January 2, 1608	
Daniel Stallings	Jeweler	January 2, 1608	
Edward Brinton	Mason	May 13, 1607	September 1608; December 29, 1608: sent to help Powhatan hunt birds, tried to warn men in James Fort of the German glassmakers' conspiracy to steal arms
Robert Alberton	Perfumer	January 2, 1608	
William Callicut (Caldicot)	Refiner	Not known	October 1608: on trip with Newport to the Monacan; looking for mines containing precious metals near Richmond
William Dawson	Refiner	January 2, 1608	Leads frenzied search for gold from January to April 10, 1608
Abram Ransack	Refiner	January 2, 1608	Leads frenzied search for gold from January to April 10, 1608
Jonas Profit	Sailer	May 13, 1607	June 2, 1608: fisher; July 20, 1608: soldier, Profit's Pool named after him; December 29, 1608: Master of the Pinnace
William Love	Tailor	May 13, 1607	December 29, 1608: soldier
Thomas Hope	Tailor	January 2, 1608	
William Ward	Tailor	January 2, 1608	July 20, 1608: soldier; December 29, 1608: soldier; Ward's Point named after him
John Powell	Tailor	January 2, 1608	June 2, 1608: soldier
William Young (Yonge)	Tailor	January 2, 1608	
William Beckwith	Tailor	January 2, 1608	
Lawrence Towtales	Tailor	January 2, 1608	
Robert Cotton	Tobacco pipemaker	January 2, 1608	

Endnotes

[1] George Percy, *Observations gathered out of "A Discourse of the Southern Colony in Virginia by the English, 1606,"* ed. David B. Quinn (Charlottesville, VA: Univ. Press of Virginia, 1967), 16.

[2] "Advice of the Council, December 10, 1606" in Alexander Brown, *The Genesis of the United States* (Boston: Houghton, Mifflin and Company, 1890), II: 81.

[3] Edmund S. Morgan, *American Slavery, American Freedom* (New York: W.W. Norton & Company, Inc., 1975), 84. Alfred J. Mapp, *The Virginia Experiment* (LaSalle, IN: Open Court, 1974) 7-8.

[4] Philip L. Barbour, ed., *The Complete Works of Captain John Smith (1580-1631)* (Chapel Hill, NC: The Univ. of North Carolina Press, 1986), II: 141. Percy, 24-27.

[5] A database of biographical information in the initial stages of developement by Catherine Correll-Walls, APVA research assistant. Tentatively entitled "First Settlers Project," it incorporates traditional Jamestown sources and goes beyond to include information accessible via the World Wide Web, including British Public Record office holdings (www.pro.gov.uk); British County records; County Genealogical Society information, including searchable Surname lists and links to Parish Registers; and Bishops' Transcripts preserved locally (www.genuki.org.uk). Other online information databases include the Royal Commission on Historical Manuscripts (www.hmc.gov.uk), the National Register of Archives (www.hmc.gov.uk/nra/nra.htm), the British Library (www.bl.uk), the University of Oxford Library (www.bodley.ox.ac.uk), the National Library of Wales (www.llgc.org.uk), the National Maritime Museum (www.rog.nmm.ac.uk). The project also includes biographical information from the Vital Records Index British Isles, Family History Resource File, CDROM and the online International Genealogical Index (www.familysearch.com) , The Church of Jesus Christ of Latter Day Saints, Dr. S. E. Sutton, "The First Virginia Colonists," report, Jamestown-Yorktown Foundation, 1988.

[6] Percy, 26.

[7] Daniel Brown alerted me to the exact numbers.

[8] William Whiffin, "Sir Walter Raleigh's House," exhibit at Tower Hamlets Local History Archives, Bancroft Library, London, photo.

[9] Alexander Brown, II: 904, 943-944, 977-978, 1006-1010, 1055. Jocelyn R. Wingfield, *Virginia's True Founder: Edward-Maria Wingfield and His Times, 1550-c.1614* (Athens, GA: The Wingfield Family Society, 1993). Samuel Merrifield Bemiss, *Ancient Adventurers, A Collection of Essays* (Richmond, VA: Garrett & Massie, 1964). Warner F. Gookin, "Who Was Bartholomew Gosnold?," *William and Mary Quarterly* 3rd Ser., 6 (1949): 401.

[10] Mary Abbott, *Life Cycles in England, 1560-1720, Cradle to Grave* (London and New York: Routledge, 1996), 135.

[11] These are all age estimates based on very preliminary research as part of the "First Settlers Project."

[12] Ibid.

[13] Nell Marion Nugent, *Cavaliers and Pioneers, abstracts of Virginia land patents and grants, 1623-1666* (Baltimore: Genealogical Publishing Co, Inc., 1974), XXI.

[14] W. Stitt Robinson, Jr., *Mother Earth Land Grants in Virginia, 1607-1699* (Williamsburg, VA: Va. 350th Anniversary Celebration Corp., 1957), passim.

[15] Martin does eventually get by grant 10 shares (1000 acres) of choice land in 1616 and stays in Virginia. This may mean his prospects for land back home were not major. Alexander Brown, II: 943.

[16] APVA, First Settlers Project.

[17] Gookin, 401.

[18] Ibid. The author is indebited to Nicholas Hagger, owner of Otley Hall, the Gosnold mansion, for suggesting sources for Gosnold's life.

[19] Barbour, I: 203.

[20] Percy, 24-25.

[21] Percy, 24-27.

[22] APVA, First Settlers Project.

[23] William M. Kelso, *Jamestown Rediscovery I* (Richmond, VA: Association for the Preservation of Virginia Antiquites, 1993), 5.

[24] Richard Randolph, "Island of Jamestown," *Southern Literary Messenger* 3 (1837): 303-304. John L. Cotter, *Archaeological Excavations at Jamestown* (Washington D.C.: National Park Service, United States Department of the Interior, 1958), 3-6.

[25] William M. Kelso, *Jamestown Rediscovery I-II* (Richmond, VA: Association for the Preservation of Virginia Antiquities, 1995, 1996), *passim*. William M. Kelso, Nicholas M. Luccketti, Beverly A. Straube, *Jamestown Rediscovery III-V* (Richmond, VA: Association for the Preservation of Virginia Antiquities, 1997, 1998, 1999), *passim*.

[26] Douglas Owsley, "Immigrants and Residents: Isotope Signatures in the Chesapeake during the Colonial Period" (paper presented at Human Remains: Conservation, Retrieval & Analysis Conference, Williamsburg, VA, November, 1999).

[27] Personal communication with Dr. Paul Budd, University of Bradford.

[28] Julian Litten, *The English Way of Death*, (London: Robert Hale Limited, 1992), 99.

[29] Owsley.

[30] Barbour, II: 211.

[31] William Strachey, "True Reportory of the Wreck and Redemption of Sir Thomas Gates, Knight" in *A Voyage to Virginia in 1609*, ed. Louis B. Wright (Charlottesville: The University of Virginia Press, 1973), 79.

[32] Barbour, II: 235-236. Strachey, 80-82.

[33] Strachey, 81.

[34] Ibid.

[35] Kelso, Luccketti, Straube, *Jamestown Rediscovery III*.

[36] Barbour, II: 180-181.

[37] Strachey, 64.

[38] Ralph Hamor, *A True Discourse of the Present Estate of Virginia* (Richmond: The Virginia State Library, 1957), 33.

[39] Dr. Joanne Bowen, "The Starving Time at Jamestown," December, 1999. Report on file with APVA.

[40] Kelso, *Jamestown Rediscovery II*. Kelso, Luccketti, Straube, *Jamestown Rediscovery III-IV*.

[41] Strachey, 41.

[42] It should be emphasized here that the Bermudan garbage may not have been deposited in the cellars in May-June 1610, but not before that date.

[43] Strachey, 75.

[44] Percy on waiting for De La Warre.

[45] Strachey, 77.

[46] Barbour, I: 259.

[47] George Percy, "A True Relation", in *Jamestown Narratives, Eyewitness Accounts of the Virginia Colony*, Edward Haile ed. (Champlain, VA: Roundhouse Publishing, 1998), 505.

[48] Agape Vets

[49] Smith's Map of Virginia, 1612, detail in Barbour, II: 140-141. Scott Weidensail, "Tracking America's First Dog," *Smithsonian Magazine*, March 1999, 45-57.

[50] Barbour, II: 350.

[51] Nancy Egloff, "Report on Starving Time Population Figures," unpublished manuscript Jamestown Yorktown Foundation, 1990. APVA, First Settlers Project.

[52] Samuel H. Yonge, *The Site Of Old "James Towne" 1607-1698* (Richmond, VA: L.H.I Jenkins, Inc., 1952), 66.

[53] Owsley for age of Rev guy and Beverly A. Straube, "An Analysis of the Buttons from Archaeological Sites at Kingsmill on the James, Virginia," unpublished ms on file (1990), 11.

[54] Patent 8, "Ambler Family Papers, 1638-1810," Library of Congress, Washington, D.C., 315.

[55] Yonge, 78. Martha W. McCartney, *James City County, Keystone of the Commonwealth* (Virginia Beach, VA: The Donning Company, 1997), 80.

[56] Yonge, 78-97.

[57] "T.M." "Bacon's Rebellion in Virginia" 13 July, 1705, in Peter Force, *Tracts and Other Papers, Relating principally To The Original Settlement, and Progress of the Colonies in North America* (Washington: Peter Force, 1886), Vol. I: 5-24.

[58] Barbour, II:239.

[59] Barbour, II:225.

[60] Brown, 83.

[61] Ibid., 83.

[62] The Ancient Planter of Virginia, "A Brief Declaration," (1623) in Haile, 894.

[63] John Smith inherited this position from Thomas Studley who died August 28, 1607.

[64] Barbour, III: 272.

[65] Philip L. Barbour, *The Jamestown Voyages Under the First Charter, 1607-1609* (Cambridge: The University Press, 1969), I: 108.

66 Ibid, I:176, Newport to Lort Salisbury, July 29, 1607.

67 Derek Keene, "Metalworking in Medieval London: an Historical Survey," *Historical Metallurgy* 30:2 (1996): 96.

68 Barbour, *John Smith,* II:157

69 Barbour, *John Smith,* II:158

70 Barbour, *John Smith,* II:184

71 Barbour, *John Smith,* III:271

72 William Waller Hening, *The Statutes at Large* (1823; facsimile reprint Charlottesville, VA: Univ. of Virginia Press, 1969), 135.

73 Justine Bayley (1996) "Innovation in Later Medieval Urban Metalworking," *The Journal of the Historical Metallurgy Society,* Volume 30, Number 2, 70.

74 Martincamp flasks found in association with evidence of metalworking at the site of the 1585 settlement on Roanoke Island, North Carolina, are believed to have been used as receivers.

75 Jacqueline Pearce, personal communication, 1999. Stephen Moorhouse "Medieval Distilling-Apparatus of Glass and Pottery," *Medieval Archaeology* VI (1972): 120.

76 Jacqueline Pearce, personal communication, 1999.

77 An earthenware alembic was excavated from an early 17th-century context at Martin's Hundred, an area adjacent to Jamestown, Ivor Noël Hume, *Martin's Hundred,* (New York, A Delta Book, 1982), 101-102.

78 Jacqueline Pearce, personal communication 1999. Moorhouse, 96-97.

79 Moorhouse, 87.

80 Campbell, 151.

81 Diana Scarisbrick, *Tudor and Jacobean Jewellery* (London: Tate Publishing, 1995), 38.

82 Barbour, *John Smith,* II:199.

83 Brown, I:83.

84 David Parsons, "Stone," *English Medieval Industries,* John Blair and Nigel Ramsey, eds. (London: The Hambledon Press, 1991), 25.

85 Barbour, *John Smith,* II:162

86 Adrian Oswald, *Clay Pipes for the Archaeologist,* British Archaeological Reports 14 (1975), 76.

87 Colin Andrew Tatam, "The Clay Tobacco Pipe Industry in the Parish of Newington, Southwark, London," in *The Archaeology of the Clay Tobacco Pipe* XIII, Ed. By Peter Davey. BAR British Series, No. 239 (1994): 5. D.J. Markell "The Clay Tobacco Pipes," in Ian P. Horsey, *Excavations in Poole 1973-1983,* (Dorchester: Dorset History and Archaeological Society, 1992), 159.

88 Oswald, 96.

89 Willliam Harrison, *Great Chronologie,* as quoted in Oswald, 3.

90 Paul Hentzner, *Itinerarium,* as quoted in Oswald, 5.

91 D. Rhodes, *Clay and Glazes for the Potter* (Pennsylvania: Chilton Book Company, 1973), 20 as quoted in Tatam, 17.

92 Adrian Oswald, "Marked Clay Pipes from Plymouth, Devon," *Post-Medieval Archaeology* 3, (1969): 138-139.

93 David Jones, Ipswich Museum, personal communication, December 1998.

94 Compact Oxford English Dictionary (Oxford: Clarendon Press, 1998), 1310:546.

95 Jacqueline Pearce, *Border Wares* (London: HMSO, 1992), 41.

96 William Shakespeare, *Much Ado About Nothing,* I. 3. 53-54.

97 Carole Rawcliffe, *Medicine and Society in Later Medieval England* (Alan Sutton Publishing, 1995), 160.

98 F.P. Wilson, *The Plague in Shakespeare's London* (Oxford: Oxford University Press, 1999), 9.

99 Eleanour Sinclair Rohde, *The Old English Herbals* (New York: Dover Publications, 1971), 72.

100 Kathleen Epstein, *British Embroidery* (Austin, Texas: Curious Works Press, 1998), 55.

101 Shakespeare, *Much Ado About Nothing,* 3. 4. 56-57.

102 Kathy Lynn Emerson, *The Writer's Guide to Everyday Life in Renaissance England* (Cincinnati, Ohio: Writer's Digest Books, 1996), 14.

103 David R. Ransome, "Wives for Virginia," *William and Mary Quarterly,* Third Series, 48, no. 1 (Jan. 1991): 16.

104 William Love arrived in May 1607 (Barbour, *John Smith,* II:142). Thomas Hope, William Ward, John Powell, William Young, William Beckwith, and Lawrence Towtales arrived in January 1608 (Barbour, *John Smith,* II:162).

105 Barbour, *John Smith,* II:170, 192.

106 Ibid, II: 172.

107 Ibid, II:155, 41.

[108] Kay Staniland, "Getting There, Got It: Archaeological Textiles and Tailoring in London, 1330-1580," *The Age of Transition*, David Gaimster and Paul Stamper, eds. (Oxford: Oxbow Books, 1997), 240.

[109] Jane Ashelford, *The Art of Dress* (London: The National Trust, 1996), 27.

[110] Francis Perkins, gentleman, arrived at Jamestown on the first supply in January 1608 along with his son Francis, whom John Smith lists as a laborer (Barbour, *John Smith*, I: 223). Within 3 days of their arrival, a fire consumed all of their possessions except a mattress that had not yet been unloaded from the ship. In a March letter written to a friend in England, he asks for 10 pounds worth of used clothing "whether it be large or small garments, doublets, trousers, stockings, capes or whatever may appear fit ... since ... everything is needed and whatever may be sent will be useful" (Brown, I: 176-177).

[111] Molina was held prisoner at Jamestown from 1611 to 1613. While there he managed to smuggle out his observations on the colony, hidden in the sole of a shoe, to the Spanish ambassador to London (Brown, II: 646).

[112] Bridget McConnel, *The Collector's Guide to Thimbles* (London: Bracken Books, 1996), 6.

[113] Randle Holme, *The Academy of Armory & Blazon, The Third Book* (Chester: Printed for the Author, 1688), 284, 290.

[114] McConnel, 10.

[115] R.F. Tylecote, "Á Contribution to the Metallurgy of 18th and 19th Century: Brass Pins," *Post-Medieval Archaeology* 6: 190.

[116] Geoff Egan and Hazel Forsyth, "Wound Wire and Silver Gilt: changing fashions in dress accessories c.1400-c.1600," in Gaimster and Stamper, 222.

[117] Chris Caple, "Factors in the Production of Medieval and Post-medieval Brass Pins," *Trade and Discovery: The Scientific Study of Artefacts from post-Medieval Europe and Beyond*, Duncan R. Hook and David R.M. Gaimster (eds.), British Museum Occasional Paper 109 (1995): 226.

[118] Starch, made of boiled wheat, was introduced into England in 1564 by Dinghen van den Plass, a Dutch woman, Ashelford, 33.

[119] John W. Shirley, "George Percy at Jamestown, 1607-1612," *The Virginia Magazine of History and Biography,* 57, no. 3 (July, 1949): 235.

[120] Barbour, *John Smith*, II: 232.

[121] Holme, 291.

[122] A parallel is depicted in the *Journal of the British Archaeological Association,* 14 (1858): 262-266.

[123] Sue Margeson, *Norwich Households: The Medieval and Post-Medieval Finds from Norwich Survey Excavations 1971-1978,* East Anglian Archaeology Report No. 58 (1993): 22.

[124] Geoff Egan, *Lead Cloth Seals and Related Items in the British Museum,* British Museum Occasional Paper 93 (1994): 1.

[125] Ibid, 4.

[126] Egan, personal communication, 1994.

[127] Shirley, 237.

[128] Brown, II: 115

[129] On at least two occasions John Smith complains about the condition of the tents that the first colonists were provided, "our Tents were rotten" (Barbour, *John Smith*, I: 35) and "in foule weather we shifted into an old rotten tent" (Ibid, III: 295).

[130] Susan M. Kingsbury, *Records of the Virginia Company* (Washington, DC: Government Printing Office, 1906), IV: 450

[131] Sheelah Ruggles-Brise, *Sealed Bottles* (New York: Charles Scribner's Sons, 1949), 162. This mark was adapted by Virginians for use on their personally marked wine bottles. Interestingly, this practice does not extend to English individuals or merchants.

[132] Robert Stenuit, "Early Relics of the VOC Trade from Shetland: The Wreck of the Flute *Lastdrager* lost off Yell, 1653," *The International Journal of Nautical Archaeology and Underwater Exploration* 3, no. 2 (1974), 243-244.

[133] Egan, *Lead Cloth Seals,* 78.

[134] Egan, personal communication, 1999.

[135] Geoff Egan, "England's Post-Medieval Cloth Trade: A Survey of the Evidence From Cloth Seals," *Trade and Discovery: The Scientific Study of Artefacts from Post-Medieval Europe and Beyond.* British Museum Occasional Paper 109 (1995): 319.

[136] Egan, *Lead Cloth Seals,* 106.

[137] Noël Hume, 190-191.

[138] Egan, "England's Post-Medieval Cloth Trade," 319.

[139] Kathy Lynn Emerson, *Everyday Life in Renaissance England From 1485-1649* (Cincinnati, Ohio: Writer's Digest Books, 1996), 22.

[140] Shirley, 237.

[141] William Shakespeare, *Taming of the Shrew*, 4.1.49.

[142] The English ell was 45 inches whereas the Dutch ell was 27 inches, Egan, *Lead Cloth Seals*, 145.

[143] Ibid, 113.

[144] Barbour, *John Smith*, III: 295.

[145] Ibid, I:263.

[146] Sassafras was believed in the 17th century to be a cure for scurvy, yellow jaundice, and the French disease (syphilis). The London surgeon John Woodall who sent a fully equipped surgeons chest to Jamestown in 1609 noted that, "the best of these rootes grow in Virginia." John Woodall, *The Surgions Mate* (1617; reprint with forward by John Kirkup, Bath: Kingsmead, 1978), 56.

[147] Brown, I:107.

[148] OED 671, 943.

[149] Gabriel Archer, "The descripton of the now-discovered river and country of Virginia, with the likelihood of ensuing riches by England's aid and industry" in Haile, 119.

[150] Brown, I:107.

[151] Edward Maria Wingfield, "A Discourse of Virginia," in Jocelyn Wingfield, 319.

[152] The Ancient Planters of Virginia, "A Brief Declaration," in Haile, 894.

[153] The London Virginia Company, "Instructions by way of advice, for the intended Voyage to Virginia," in Jocelyn Wingfield, 295.

[154] Barbour, *John Smith*, II:225.

[155] Wingfield, "A Discourse" in Jocelyn Wingfield: 327.

[156] Barbour, *John Smith*, I:41.

[157] Ibid, II:172.

[158] William Thorndale, "Drew Pickayes (1564-1607)" *The American Genealogist*. 70:3, No. 279:131-132.

[159] Thorndale, 225

[160] Barbour, *John Smith*, II:189.

[161] Ibid, I:35.

[162] In 1986 a socketed chisel was successfully produced in an experimental bloomery using limonite derived from surface deposits within 20 miles of Jamestown, David Harvey, "Reconstructing the American Bloomery Process," *The Colonial Williamsburg Historic Trades Annual*, I: 19-37.

[163] Howard B. Gill, "The Blacksmith in Colonial Virginia," Unpublished ms on file, Colonial Williamsburg Foundation, 1965, 6-7.

[164] Gill, 110.

[165] This work, called Project 100, was initiated by the National Park Service to find evidence of the first fort. The conclusions were that no trace had been found, John L. Cotter, *Archeological Excavations at Jamestown, Virginia*, Second Edition, Special Publication no. 32 (Richmond, VA: Archeological Society of Virginia, 1994), 11-17.

[166] Gill, 109.

[167] William M. Kelso, Nicholas M. Luccketti, and Beverly A. Straube, "A Re-Evaluation of the Archaeological Evidence Produced by Project 100," Unpublished ms submitted to Colonial National Historical Park, 1990.

[168] Brown, I:328.

[169] Barbour, *John Smith*, II: 311.

[170] David B. Quinn. *The Roanoke Voyages 1584-1590* (London: Hakluyt Society, 1955), 831.

[171] Barbour, *John Smith*, II:225.

[172] J. C. Harrington, *A Tryal of Glasse* (Richmond, VA: The Dietz Press, 1980), 10. Charles E. Hatch, "Glassmaking in Virginia, 1607-1625," *William and Mary College Quarterly* Second Series, 21, no. 2 (April 1941): 128-129.

[173] Barbour, *John Smith*, II:191.

[174] Ibid, II:190.

[175] Ibid, II:181.

[176] Germany, particularly the area of the Kaufunger Wald in the northern part of the County of Hesse, was well known for its glass production in the 16th and 17th centuries. On the other hand, the Baltic areas of Poland were England's sources of pitch and tar in this period. In addition, references to glass production at Jamestown ceases after 1610, by which time the Germans are dead, whereas pitch, tar, and soap ashes continue to be exported to England.

[177] Eleanor S. Godfrey, *The Development of English Glassmaking 1560-1640* (Chapel Hill: The University of North Carolina Press, 1975), 212.

[178] Potash was a rare and costly commodity in 17th-century England and

glassmakers had to compete for it with other industries such as the making of soap and saltpeter.

[179] Godfrey, 204.

[180] Godfrey, 160.

[181] This identification was made by Dr. Brent E. Owens, Geology Department, College of William and Mary.

[182] Vannoccio Biringuccio, *The Pirotechnia*. (Boston: The M.I.T. Press, 1959), 113.

[183] There are residual deposits of pyrolusite in Augusta and Shenandoah counties in Virginia but there was no mining done in these areas during the early colonial period (Charles Palache et al., *The System of Mineralogy of James Dwight Dana and Edward Salisbury Dana*. 5th ed. (New York: John Wiley and Sons, Inc., 1951), I: 564.

[184] Hans-Georg Stephan, personal communication, 1998, Hans-Georg Stephan, *Grossalmerode*. (Grossalmerode: Glas-und Keramikmuseum Grossalmerode, 1995), 44, Figures 24 and 25.

[185] Harrington, *passim*.

[186] Barbour, *John Smith*, II: 192.

[187] Ibid, I: lxi.

[188] Ibid, I: 221.

[189] Brown, II: 799.

Illustration Credits

Figure 1. Algemeen Rijksarchief, Den Haag, Netherlands.

Figure 3. John Speed, *A Tudor Atlas*. By permission of the British Library, London.

Figure 4. *Sir Walter Raleigh's House, 1873,* William Whiffin Collection, Tower Hamlets Local History Archives, Bancroft Library, London.

Figure 10. Copyright David Doody.

Figure 13. Robert Vaugn (after John White), *John Smith takes the King of the Pamaunke Prisoner,* 1608, Grenville Kane Collection. Department of Rare Books and Special Collections. Princeton University Library.

Figure 17. Detail, *Vingboon Atlas*, Algemeen Rijksarchief, Den Haag, Netherlands.

Figure 22. John Speed, *A Tudor Atlas*. By permission of the British Library, London.

Figure 23. *Fort St. George*, Archivo General de Simancas (Ministerio de Educacion y Cultura de Espana). MPD XIX-163.

Figure 24. "Jamestown 1619 by Sidney King," National Park Service, Colonial National Historical Park.

Figure 28. Detail, John Smith/William Hole, *Map of Virginia* (first state), Virginia Historical Society, Richmond, Virginia.

Figure 34. Jan Steen, *Skittle-players outside an Inn*, National Gallery, London.

Figure 35, 41, 50, 52, 53, 58, 61, 70, 71, 74. From Randle Holme, *The Academy of Armory & Blazon, The Third Book* (Chester: Printed for the Author, 1688).

Figure 36. Cornelis Bega, *The Alchemist*, 84.PB.56, The J. Paul Getty Museum, Los Angeles.

Figure 44. Andrian Brouwer, *The Smokers,* The Metropolitan Museum of Art, The Friedsam Collection, Bequest of Michael Friedsam, 1931.(32.100.21), Photograph © 1989 The Metropolitan Museum of Art.

Figure 45. Hendrick Terbrugghen, *Boy Lighting His Pipe with a Candle*, Dobo Itsvan Varmuzeum, Eger, Electa Archive, Milano.

Figure 47. Tudor earthenware fuming pot, IT.328, Picture Library, Museum of London.

Figure 49. Jan Steen, *The Lovesick Girl*, Electa Archive, Milano.

Figure 51. Quiringh van Brekelenkam, *Interior of a Tailor's Shop,* National Gallery, London.

Figure 60. Anthony van Dyck, *Portrait of a Man*, The Metropolitan Museum of Art, Marquand Collection, Gift of Henry G. Marquand, 1889.(89.15.11), Photograph © 1984, The Metropolitan Museum of Art.

Figure 64. British School, *William Style of Langley*, 1636, Tate Gallery, London/ Art Resources, New York.

Figure 76. Gabriel Metsu, *The Interior of a Smithy*, National Gallery, London.

Figure 80. *A Diderot Pictorial Encyclopedia of Trades and Industry,* Charles C. Gillispie, ed., (New York: Dover Publications, Inc., 1993) Plate 245, Crown Glass XI.

Figure 81. Specimen of crown glass, c. 19th century, Science Museum/Science & Society Picture Library, London.

Jamestown VI
REDISCOVERY

William M. Kelso   Beverly A. Straube

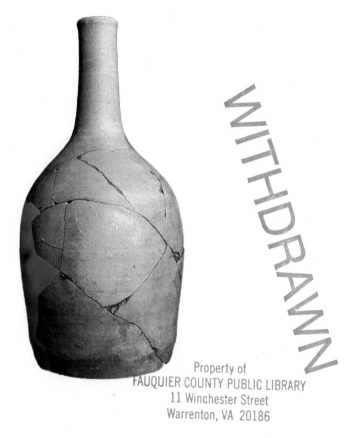

The Association for the Preservation
of Virginia Antiquities
2000

Dedication

To the Adventures of the Virginia Company.

Graphics by Jamie E. May
Design and production by Elliott Jordan

Printed in The United States of America

ISBN: 0-917565-10-X